500+ SUPER FUN AND MIND-BLOWING HOCKEY FACTS FOR KIDS:

Amazing Achievements, Comic Traditions, Inspiring Stories, and More!

Introduction

Welcome to the ultimate collection of ice hockey fun! This book is packed with over 500 amazing facts about the coolest game on Earth. Whether you're a die-hard hockey fan or just starting to learn about the sport, you're about to dive into an exciting world filled with jaw-dropping stats, hilarious stories, inspiring moments, and quirky traditions.

Hockey has a rich and fascinating history that spans the globe. From frozen ponds to grand arenas, the sport has brought people together in some of the most unique places on Earth. It's a game that welcomes everyone—whether you're tall or short, big or small, there's a place for you on the ice. Some of the greatest players of all time began their journeys when they were your age, just grabbing a stick and dreaming big.

This book is more than just a collection of facts—it's an invitation to explore, laugh, and be inspired. If you find something particularly interesting, why not look it up? The internet is full of stories about the players, teams, coaches, and unforgettable games that have shaped hockey history.

And remember: hockey isn't just about winning. It's about having fun, being a good teammate, and embracing the spirit of the game. Every hockey player starts as a beginner, but with passion and perseverance, they grow into legends. Maybe someday, we'll be writing fun facts about YOU!

Here's a little taste of what makes hockey so special:

- It's played all over the world, from icy mountains to tropical islands.
- The game is full of unique traditions and funny superstitions that players follow for good luck.
- No matter where you come from, you can be part of the hockey community—it's like one big family!

So, lace up your skates, grab your stick, and get ready to celebrate the incredible game of hockey. Let's hit the ice and start exploring 500+ reasons why hockey is the greatest sport on Earth!

The first game of ice hockey was played on a frozen pond in Montreal, Canada, in 1875. The players used sticks, a wooden puck, and made their own rules since organized ice hockey didn't exist yet.

Ice hockey originally had nine players per team on the ice at once. That's three more than today's game, which has six players per team: three forwards, two defensemen, and a goalie.

The Stanley Cup, the most famous trophy in hockey, was first awarded in 1893. It's named after Lord Stanley of Preston, the Governor General of Canada at the time, who was a huge hockey fan. Teams get their names engraved on the Cup if they win, creating a long history on the trophy itself.

Wayne Gretzky, often called "The Great One," holds the record for the most points in NHL history—2,857 points in 1,487 games! He scored so many goals and assists that no one has even come close to breaking his record.

Early hockey pucks weren't always the rubber discs we know today. Before modern pucks were invented, players used frozen cow poop or wooden blocks. Imagine how smelly that would be!

A hockey puck can travel at speeds over 100 miles per hour when hit by a professional player. The fastest slap shots, like those from **Zdeno Chára**, can even top 110 mph, making it dangerous for goalies.

Zdeno Chára holds the record for the fastest slap shot, clocking in at an incredible 118.3 miles per hour during the 2012 NHL All-Star Game skills competition. His towering height (6'9") helps him generate extra power.

The nickname "frozen pond" for a hockey rink comes from the fact that many young players start playing outdoors, on frozen lakes and ponds, before joining organized teams.

The Zamboni is an ice-resurfacing machine that makes the ice smooth between periods. It was invented by **Frank Zamboni** in 1949, and modern versions still bear his name. Without it, the ice would be rough and bumpy.

Hockey players are famous for their superstitions. Former goalie **Patrick Roy** believed that talking to his goalposts during games would bring him good luck. He even treated them like teammates! Read on for more fun hockey superstitions!

Hockey sticks are usually made of carbon fiber or composite material these days, making them super light and strong. Long ago, they were made mostly of wood! A high-quality composite stick can cost $200 to $300 (US dollars), but cheaper wooden sticks are still available for beginners.

NHL games consist of three periods, each 20 minutes long. In the early days, hockey games had two 30-minute halves, but they switched to three periods to allow for ice maintenance.

Connor McDavid of the **Edmonton Oilers** is known for his lightning-fast skating. In 2024, he was crowned the fastest skater in the NHL All-Star Game's skills competition for the fourth time!

Unlike most sports, hockey players can change lines on the fly, meaning they swap players during the game without stopping play. It adds an extra layer of strategy because players must time their shifts just right.

Women's ice hockey was added to the Winter Olympics in 1998. Team USA won the first-ever gold medal, and their fierce rivalry with Canada has been one of the sport's most exciting matchups ever since.

The largest crowd to ever watch a hockey game was over 104,000 people! It happened at Michigan Stadium in 2010 during an outdoor game between the University of Michigan and Michigan State. That's more people than you'd find in some entire towns!

Finland hosts a unique tournament called the World Ice Hockey Championships for Seniors, where players over 35 compete. It's a chance for older players to relive their glory days on the ice.

During the COVID pandemic, players had to stop high-fiving each other after goals or wins because of safety rules during the pandemic, so they invented cool air high-fives or fist bumps with gloves instead!

Gordie Howe, known as "Mr. Hockey," played in the NHL across five decades, from the 1940s to the 1980s. He played until the age of 52, making him one of the oldest professional hockey players ever.

Ice hockey was originally played with a ball instead of a puck. But because the ball would often bounce too much on the ice, the switch to a flat puck was made in the late 1800s.

Goalies wear the most protective gear on the team. Their leg pads, chest protectors, masks, and catching gloves are all designed to help them block pucks flying at speeds up to 100 miles per hour!

Goalie saves can be creative, too! Some goalies "stack their pads," lying down and putting their legs on top of each other to block low shots. It's a flashy, old-school move that still works today.

The National Hockey League (NHL) is made up of 32 teams from the United States and Canada. There are also other professional leagues worldwide, like the Kontinental Hockey League (KHL) in Russia and the Liiga in Finland.

Sidney Crosby, captain of the **Pittsburgh Penguins**, is one of the greatest players of his generation. He's won the Stanley Cup three times and earned two Olympic gold medals with Team Canada.

Funny superstition: **Sidney Crosby** wears the same athletic cup he's had since high school - even though he can certainly afford a new one! His teammates think it's pretty gross, but he won't change it.

Players sent to the penalty box for breaking the rules sit in the "sin bin," a special area off the ice. It's like being put in timeout, and their team has to play short-handed until the penalty ends.

In Iceland, they built a hockey rink inside a volcano! Well, not really - but it's in a building designed to look like one.

Hockey sticks are made from different materials, including wood, fiberglass, and carbon fiber. The choice of stick can affect how a player shoots, passes, and handles the puck. Some players are very particular about their stick's feel.

Players' hockey sticks are extremely personalized - they can choose from 87 different curves for their blades. Some players are so particular, they can tell if their stick is just 1/16 of an inch off!

Did you know that hockey legend **Don Cherry**, famous for his colorful suits and bold personality, started his career as a player before becoming one of the most famous TV commentators? He coached the **Boston Bruins** in the NHL and even had a pet dog named **Blue** who became a TV star alongside him! Don Cherry's wild outfits and love for the game made him unforgettable.

Some players NEVER touch the Stanley Cup until they win it! They think if they touch it before winning, they'll jinx their chances forever.

During the 2020 season, most stadiums were closed to the public due to the COVID-19 pandemic. To make empty arenas look more fun, some places filled the seats with cardboard cutouts or even virtual fans, creating a funny but creative solution!

The **Buffalo Sabres**' mascot, **Sabretooth**, is a giant bison who pumps up the crowd by leading chants, dancing, and even skating with the players during games.

Icing is a rule that stops players from shooting the puck too far down the ice without anyone touching it. It's used to keep the game moving and prevent teams from just dumping the puck to waste time.

◆

Former **New York Rangers** goalie **Henrik Lundqvist** wasn't just known for his skills in net—he's also known for his sharp sense of fashion. Nicknamed "King Henrik," he's often seen dressed in stylish suits off the ice. He was also a guitar player in a rock band when he wasn't stopping pucks, which earned him the alternate nickname "The Rock Star Goalie!"

Hockey player **Theo Fleury** was one of the smallest players ever at 5'6" (168 cm), but he scored over 1,000 points in his career!

There's a hockey team in Kenya! They practice on inline skates because there's no ice rink, but they dream of competing in the Winter Olympics someday.

Cam Neely, the hockey legend, was so good at scoring goals that he earned the nickname **"Bam-Bam Cam"** because of his hard-hitting style and powerful plays! He played for the **Boston Bruins** and became one of the best power forwards in NHL history. Oh, and here's something cool—he also acted in the movie *Dumb and Dumber*! Keep an eye out for him playing a funny character named "Sea Bass."

Canada is considered the birthplace of hockey, and Canadian teams like the **Montreal Canadiens** and **Toronto Maple Leafs** have some of the most devoted fan bases in the sport. Hockey is more than just a game there—it's part of the culture!

The Hockey Hall of Fame in Toronto celebrates the greatest players and moments in the history of the sport. It's also home to the original Stanley Cup, as well as the current Stanley Cup Trophy where fans can see the names of legendary players engraved on it and even have their photo taken with it! Visitors can also try their hand at hockey skills in interactive zones!

It's common for NHL players to be missing front teeth. Hockey is a rough sport, and pucks, sticks, and even other players can knock teeth out. Some players wear mouthguards, but it's not mandatory. Some players don't even bother getting fake ones until they retire because they might just lose them again!

The Netherlands has a hockey team that plays on frozen canals in winter. They clear the ice early in the morning before boats need to use it!

Fans of the **Detroit Red Wings** have a quirky tradition during playoff games. They throw octopuses onto the ice! The tradition began in 1952 when eight wins were needed to win the Stanley Cup (each octopus has eight arms). In fact, "**Al the Octopus**" is the team's mascot!

Some players put their skates in the oven (at a very low temperature) to help mold them to their feet. Don't try this at home!

In Croatia, there's a hockey tournament played on a frozen lake where teams can only use wooden sticks made from local trees.

The Miracle on Ice is one of the most famous hockey stories in history. In the 1980 Winter Olympics, the underdog U.S. team, made up of amateur and collegiate players, shocked the world by defeating the heavily favored Soviet Union team, considered unbeatable at the time. The U.S. went on to win the gold medal, in what is considered one of the greatest moments in sports history.

Roy "Shrimp" Worters, who stood at just 5'3", was the shortest player in NHL history. Despite his small size, he was a talented goalie and even won the Hart Trophy, awarded to the league's most valuable player.

Professional hockey sticks are customized for players' height and preferences. They're usually between 50 and 65 inches long, depending on the player's size. Many pro players name their sticks or have personal signatures on them. It's a way to connect with their gear for good luck during games!

South Korean player **Park Jong-ah** learned to play hockey in less than five years and made it to the Olympics! Her teammates call her "Lightning Park."

Hockey skate blades are curved, not flat! They're actually shaped like a very shallow "U" so that only about 1-2 inches of the blade touches the ice at any time. This is called the "rocker" and helps players make quick turns.

Pavel Datsyuk of the **Detroit Red Wings** was known as "The Magic Man" because of his mind-blowing stickhandling abilities. His highlight-reel plays are still watched by fans all over the world.

The **Vancouver Canucks** have a fan who plays "Johnny Canuck" - he grows a real lumberjack beard and wears plaid to every game!

◆

Alex Ovechkin of the **Washington Capitals** is one of the best goal-scorers in hockey history. He's scored over 800 goals in his career and is known for his powerful one-timer from the left faceoff circle, often called his "office." He continues to chase **Wayne Gretzky**'s all-time goal record.

In European leagues like the Swedish Hockey League (SHL), the rink is wider than in the NHL. This gives players more space to skate and makes for a faster, more wide-open style of play.

Ice hockey is popular around the world, with leagues in over 70 countries. Countries with cold climates dominate, but there are even teams in warmer places like Mexico, Australia, and Israel!

Hockey players wrap their sticks with either black or white tape, depending on their preference. Some use black tape to "hide" the puck from goalies, while others like white tape because it makes it easier to see the puck.

Jaromír Jágr, a legendary player from the Czech Republic, played professional hockey until his late 40s. He's the second-highest scorer in NHL history (after **Wayne Gretzky**) and in 2024 became the oldest player to score a professional goal at age 52!

In the NHL, each player can only wear a unique number on their jersey. Once a player chooses their number, no one else on the team can wear it. Some famous numbers, like **Wayne Gretzky's** #99, are retired across the entire league.

Outdoor games, like the Winter Classic, have become a fan favorite. Teams play in open-air stadiums in front of huge crowds, and sometimes it even snows during the game!

P.K. Subban, a former defenseman for the **Montreal Canadiens** and **Nashville Predators**, is not only known for his skills but also for his big personality. A trailblazer in the NHL as a prominent Black player, he's also done a lot of charity work, including donating millions to children's hospitals.

The Chinese national team has a player who learned to play hockey by watching YouTube videos! Now she teaches other kids the same way.

Goalie pads used to be stuffed with deer hair because it was water-resistant and kept its shape. Today, they use special foams that are lighter but provide better protection.

The Stanley Cup weighs 34.5 pounds, making it one of the heaviest trophies in sports. When a team wins it, each player gets to lift the Cup and skate around the rink in celebration.

Conor Bedard was the number one draft pick in the 2023 NHL Draft by the **Chicago Blackhawks**. He is a very superstitious player who doesn't like his stick blade to touch the ground so he keeps his stick upside-down in the rack!

Nigerian hockey player **Jujhar Khaira** learned to play in a barn in Canada. Now he inspires kids in both countries to try hockey!

During the playoffs, many players grow a "playoff beard" for good luck. They start growing it when the playoffs begin and don't shave until their team is eliminated — or they win the Stanley Cup. Some players won't shave on game days. Others won't shave at all during winning streaks. The record for "longest lucky beard" was set by **Brent Burns** - it looked like a bird's nest!

Yūjirō Konno was one of the first Japanese players to make it to the NHL. Although he didn't play many games, his success helped inspire a new generation of Japanese hockey players.

The world's northernmost hockey game was played at the North Pole in 2019! The players had to watch out for polar bears!

The **Montreal Canadiens** are the most successful NHL team, with 24 Stanley Cup championships. Their last win was in 1993, but they remain one of the most historic and beloved teams in hockey.

Players from all over the world come to the NHL, making it one of the most international sports leagues. Countries like Sweden, Russia, Finland, and the Czech Republic produce some of the league's top players.

A.J. Mleczko won an Olympic gold medal AND became one of the first women to be a regular NHL TV announcer!

Each hockey skate blade has TWO edges (inside and outside), like a tiny valley running along the bottom. Players can shift their weight to use either edge, which is how they can stop so quickly and make sharp turns. Figure skates only use one edge at a time!

The Gordie Howe Hat Trick is a special achievement where a player scores a goal, gets an assist, and gets into a fight—all in one game. **Gordie Howe**, known for both his scoring and toughness, made this feat famous.

The Stanley Cup has its own bodyguard! Since the trophy is so valuable, it travels with a handler from the Hockey Hall of Fame who makes sure it stays safe and secure. The bodyguard also makes sure the Cup isn't damaged or lost!

One of the wildest traditions in hockey involves throwing hats on the ice! When a player scores three goals in one game, it's called a "hat trick," and fans celebrate by tossing their hats onto the ice. It's a big honor for the player—and a lot of fun for fans.

Hockey players are known for their incredible stamina, and many train their entire lives for the NHL. **Sidney Crosby** began playing hockey at just 2 years old, using a small stick in his family's basement. By the time he was 7, he was already dominating local leagues in his hometown of Cole Harbour, Nova Scotia. But it's never too late to get started!

Many goalies HATE it when anyone touches their equipment. They think someone else's hand prints will let pucks sneak through!

The Japanese ice hockey league has a team that's owned by a paper company. Their jerseys are made from recycled paper products!

The **Los Angeles Kings**' mascot, **Bailey** the lion, wears the number 72, representing the average temperature in LA—far from freezing! Bailey is known for his pranks on opposing teams and his wild antics to fire up the crowd.

"The Goal" by **Bobby Orr** in the 1970 Stanley Cup Finals is one of the most famous moments in hockey history. Orr scored the game-winning goal for the **Boston Bruins** while flying through the air after being tripped by a defender. The photo of him suspended in mid-air became legendary.

Ice hockey is the fastest team sport in the world. Players often reach speeds of 20 miles per hour while skating, and the puck can move even faster—up to 100 miles per hour!

The Desert Diamond Arena, home of the now-disbanded **Arizona Coyotes**, is located in the desert! Even though Arizona is known for its extremely hot weather, the Coyotes played indoors on an ice rink kept cold by super powerful cooling systems. The locals loved coming in out of the heat and regularly filled the arena for home games! Many new hockey fans were created during the Coyotes' existence, including current All-Star forward **Auston Matthews**, who knew after watching just one game as a kid that hockey was the sport for him!

Hockey legend **Mark Messier** once ordered pizza for everyone in Madison Square Garden when the power went out during a game!

The Israeli women's national team practices year-round even though they only have one ice rink in the whole country!

The blade of a hockey stick has a curve to help players shoot and control the puck better. The curve can be slight or dramatic, depending on the player's style.

◆

Teemu Selänne, known as "The Finnish Flash," holds the record for the most goals scored by a rookie in NHL history with 76 goals in the 1992-93 season. He went on to become one of the greatest players from Finland, winning the Stanley Cup and multiple Olympic medals.

◆

Hockey player **Andrew Ference** used to compost at the arena and rode his bike to games to help the environment. His teammates called him "Captain Planet!"

◆

NHL players get their skates sharpened before EVERY game! The sharpness is measured by something called the "hollow" - some players like really sharp skates for quick turns, while others prefer less sharp ones for more gliding speed.

Many hockey teams have goal songs that blast through the arena when they score. For example, the **Chicago Blackhawks** play "Chelsea Dagger" by The Fratellis, a tune that's instantly recognizable to fans.

The "Ebug" story of **David Ayres** in 2020 is one of the most heartwarming moments in NHL history. Ayres, a 42-year-old Zamboni driver, was called into an NHL game as an emergency backup goalie for the **Carolina Hurricanes**. Despite not being a professional player, Ayres made several key saves and helped the Hurricanes win the game!

The **Toronto Maple Leafs** were once called the **Toronto St. Patricks**. They changed their name to the Maple Leafs in 1927, and on St. Patrick's Day, they sometimes wear their old green jerseys to honor their original team name.

In 1991, a player named **Gilbert Dionne** scored a goal with a puck that had been chewed by his dog! The puck had teeth marks on it!

The Winter Classic is an annual outdoor hockey game held on New Year's Day. It takes place in iconic stadiums, such as Wrigley Field in Chicago and Fenway Park in Boston. It's one of the most watched and celebrated games of the season.

In Sweden, the term for a "hat trick" is a bit different. It's called a "läckert", which roughly translates to "a sweet move" or "nice play." The tradition of throwing hats on the ice has even spread to some European leagues!

Alex Ovechkin became the first Russian-born player to captain an NHL team to a Stanley Cup victory when the **Washington Capitals** won in 2018. Ovechkin also broke the record for most goals scored by a Russian player, surpassing **Sergei Fedorov's** 483-goal mark.

Some hockey teams have unique pregame rituals. **The Calgary Flames** enter their home ice through a giant, fiery "C" tunnel, complete with real flames shooting up to get the crowd pumped up.

The **Hanson Brothers** from the movie "Slap Shot" were real hockey players! They just played themselves and didn't have to act much.

In India, some teams practice on roller skates during the summer so they can keep playing when there's no ice!

Hockey Hall of Famer **Maurice "Rocket" Richard** was known for his intense style of play and blazing speed. He was the first player to ever score 50 goals in 50 games, a feat that has only been accomplished a handful of times since.

Hockey goalies often have custom-painted masks that show off their personalities. **Marc-André Fleury,** a goalie for the **Minnesota Wild** in the NHL, has been known for his flashy, colorful masks featuring everything from knights to dragons, and always feature a fleur-de-lis on the backplate and the initials EFGT to honor his four grandparents.

The first women's professional hockey league was founded in 2015 as the National Women's Hockey League (NWHL). Since then, women's hockey has grown rapidly, with leagues and tournaments around the world gaining more attention. In 2023, the Professional Women's Hockey League had its first season in North America, and during the season the league broke the attendance record for professional women's hockey multiple times!

Pro hockey players' skates can cost over $1,000 (USD) a pair! But they're so lightweight that each skate only weighs about as much as a can of soup, even though they're super strong.

Some players think it's bad luck to use tape that isn't white or black on their sticks. But **Alexander Ovechkin** uses bright blue tape and he scores lots of goals!

The Hart Memorial Trophy is awarded each year to the NHL's most valuable player (MVP). Some players, like

Wayne Gretzky, have won it multiple times—Gretzky holds the record with nine Hart Trophy wins!

◆

Hockey players have a tradition called "taping their sticks." They wrap the blades of their sticks in cloth tape, usually in black or white. It helps them grip the puck better and protects the stick from wear and tear.

◆

In the early 2000s, the **Detroit Red Wings** were nick-named the "Russian Five" because they had five star Russian players—**Sergei Fedorov, Slava Fetisov, Igor Larionov, Vladimir Konstantinov**, and **Slava Kozlov**—who dominated the NHL with their slick passing and teamwork.

During the 2017 playoffs between the **Ottawa Senators** and the **Boston Bruins,** a fan threw a pink beach ball onto the ice. The referee picked it up and hilariously hid it under the back of his jersey, continuing to skate as if nothing had happened!

Finnish player **Michelle Karvinen** has special hockey skates designed for people with different leg lengths - proving anyone can play hockey!

The Conn Smythe Trophy is awarded to the MVP of the Stanley Cup Playoffs, not the regular season. Many players consider it one of the highest honors in hockey because it rewards peak performance when it matters most—in the playoffs!

About 60% of hockey players use a left-handed stick, even if they're right-handed in daily life! It depends on what feels more natural to them on the ice.

Hockey goalie masks weren't always a thing. In fact, goalies used to play without any face protection! **Jacques Plante** was the first goalie to regularly wear a mask in 1959 after taking a puck to the face. It was actually against the rules to wear a mask back then, but Plante bent the rules in favor of safety. Today, no goalie would ever step on the ice without one!

The longest NHL winning streak belongs to the **Pittsburgh Penguins**, who won 17 games in a row during the 1992-1993 season. Led by **Mario Lemieux**, the Penguins dominated the league that year.

The Australian women's national team is nicknamed the "Ice Roos" - like kangaroos, but on ice!

The blade on a hockey skate isn't just one piece of metal - it's actually two parts: the blade holder (the plastic part attached to the boot) and the steel runner that can be removed and replaced when it gets too worn down.

Hockey players sometimes wear special uniforms during warm-ups to honor causes like cancer research or military veterans. These jerseys are often auctioned off after the game, with proceeds going to charity.

Jonathan Toews, former captain of the **Chicago Blackhawks**, has won three Stanley Cups and two Olympic gold medals with Team Canada. Known for his leadership, Toews earned the nickname "Captain Serious" for his focused, no-nonsense approach to the game.

Montreal Canadiens fans think it's good luck to sing "Ole, Ole, Ole" during games. If they start singing too early, other fans shush them so they don't jinx it!

In 1999, the NHL introduced the "two-line pass rule", allowing for more exciting, fast-paced play. Before this rule change, players couldn't pass the puck across two blue lines, which slowed the game down.

◆

Wayne Gretzky's first NHL game was on October 10, 1979, for the **Edmonton Oilers**. He didn't score a goal in his debut, but by the end of his career, he had scored 894 goals, more than any player in history.

Hockey player **Dominik Hasek** was so flexible that other players nicknamed him "The Elastic Man." He could do splits to stop the puck!

The **Buffalo Sabres** were founded in 1970, and their team name comes from the famous long, curved sword, the "sabre." Their logo features a bison and crossed sabres, a nod to both Buffalo's history and their fierce fighting spirit.

Mats Sundin was the first Swedish player to be drafted #1 overall in the NHL. He went on to have an incredible career, scoring over 500 goals and becoming the first European captain of the **Toronto Maple Leafs**.

Hockey skate boots are much stiffer than figure skates because they need to protect players' feet from flying pucks and sticks. They're made with layers of super-strong materials like carbon fiber and ballistic nylon.

Herb Brooks, coach of the 1980 "Miracle on Ice" U.S. Olympic team, was known for his motivational speeches. Before the game against the Soviet Union, he famously told his team, "Great moments are born from great opportunity." His words helped inspire the team to one of the biggest upsets in sports history.

The Lady Byng Memorial Trophy is awarded to the player who combines sportsmanship, gentlemanly conduct, and excellent playing ability. **Wayne Gretzky** won it five times, and **Red Kelly** and **Pavel Datsyuk** have each won it four times. The winner for the 2023-24 season was **Jaccob Slavin** of the **Carolina Hurricanes**, and it's the second time he has won it.

Dustin Byfuglien, a massive 6'5" defenseman known for his hard hits, is one of the few players to have won the Stanley Cup both as a forward and a defenseman. He helped the **Chicago Blackhawks** win the Cup in 2010.

Goalies sometimes "freeze the puck" by covering it with their glove to stop play. This allows their team to regroup, and a faceoff follows, giving both teams a chance to reset.

Hockey players practice a special move called a "toe drag," where they use the toe of their stick to pull the puck around an opponent. It's a tricky but impressive maneuver that can leave defenders completely fooled.

The first outdoor hockey game played by NHL teams took place in 2003 between the **Montreal Canadiens** and the **Edmonton Oilers**. Known as the Heritage Classic, it was played in freezing weather, but over 57,000 fans came out to watch!

Team Japan's goalie **Nana Fujimoto** designed a Hello Kitty mask that became so popular they made toy versions of it!

Steve Yzerman, longtime captain of the **Detroit Red Wings**, played in the NHL for over two decades and led his team to three Stanley Cup championships. Known for his leadership, Yzerman was one of the most respected captains in hockey history.

The NHL uses 40-50 pucks per game because the pucks get so cold they can crack! Pucks are kept in a freezer before games to make sure they slide smoothly on the ice.

The Mark Messier Leadership Award is named after the legendary captain who led the **New York Rangers** to their first Stanley Cup in 54 years. The award is given to players who show exceptional leadership on and off the ice.

Phil Kessel is known as one of the NHL's "iron men" because of his incredible streak of over 1,000 consecutive games played, holding the NHL record! Kessel's durability and skill make him a key player, and his love for hot dogs earned him a funny reputation among fans.

The Finnish hockey team won their first-ever Olympic gold medal in 2022. Finland's victory was a proud moment for a country where ice hockey is the national sport, cementing their status as one of the world's top hockey powers.

The **Vancouver Canucks** once had a player who would do a backflip on the ice after every win! His name was **Tiger Williams.** Williams would also celebrate his goals by riding his stick across the ice like a horse! This quirky and iconic celebration has become one of the most memorable in hockey history.

Some teams won't let anyone step on their logo on the locker room floor. They think it's super disrespectful and will bring bad luck to the whole team.

Before the invention of the Zamboni machine, it would take up to 15 people to clean the ice between periods! Now just one operator can clean and resurface the ice in minutes!

Hockey players wear a lot of gear to protect themselves, including shin guards, shoulder pads, and helmets. Some players have even been known to customize their gear for extra comfort or style, like adding extra padding or painting their helmets.

Patrick Kane, a star for the **Chicago Blackhawks** and **Detroit Red Wings**, is known for his amazing stick-handling abilities. He often uses quick moves and tricks to get around defenders and create scoring chances. Kane has won multiple Stanley Cups and an MVP award.

Most NHL players wear their skates 1-2 sizes smaller than their regular shoes! This gives them better control because their feet can't slip around inside the skate.

The **Toledo Walleye** have a "Zombie Night" where players wear jerseys that look torn and bloodied - but it's just paint!

The World Junior Ice Hockey Championships is an annual tournament featuring the best young players under 20 years old from around the world. Countries like Canada, Sweden, and Russia have won many titles, and it's a showcase of future NHL stars.

More funny superstitions: **Carey Price**, the **Montreal Canadiens** goalie, has a habit of always putting on his equipment in the same order before games. Many players believe these routines help them stay focused.

Manon Rhéaume was the first woman to play in an NHL game. She was a goalie for the Tampa Bay Lightning during a preseason game in 1992, breaking barriers for women in professional sports.

Many players won't let anyone else sharpen their skates - they think another person's energy might make them trip!

The NHL's longest game happened in 1936 between the **Detroit Red Wings** and the **Montreal Maroons**. The game lasted for 176 minutes and 30 seconds, with six overtimes, before the Red Wings finally scored the winning goal.

In Brazil, they have "Beach Hockey" tournaments during the summer using plastic ice! It's like regular hockey but you can wear shorts.

Hockey is known for its high-energy atmosphere, and sometimes mascots add to the excitement. **Gritty**, the **Philadelphia Flyers'** orange, googly-eyed mascot, has become one of the most famous mascots in sports due to his wild antics and unique look.

The fastest goal in NHL history was scored just five seconds into a game! **Doug Smail** of the **Winnipeg Jets** set the record in 1981. The puck barely hit the ice before Smail darted in and snapped a shot past the goalie. It's a record that hasn't been broken in over 40 years!

Henrik Lundqvist, a legendary goalie for the **New York Rangers**, was known as "The King." He played in over 800 NHL games, earned 60 career shutouts, and was so good in pressure situations that he became known for his incredible consistency in the playoffs.

In Poland, there's a youth hockey program where kids learn math by calculating shot angles and physics on the ice!

The Montreal Forum, where the **Montreal Canadiens** played for decades, is considered by many to be the most famous hockey arena ever. Built in 1924, it hosted countless historic moments, including over 20 Stanley

Cup Finals. Even today, the Forum is seen as a temple of hockey history.

Al MacInnis, one of the hardest-shooting defensemen in NHL history, had a slap shot that could clock in at over 100 miles per hour. Goalies dreaded facing MacInnis, who could score from the blue line with just the power of his shot. His cannon-like slap shot helped him win the Conn Smythe Trophy in 1989.

Hockey player **Paul Bissonnette** would only use white tape on his stick because he thought the colored tape was bad luck.

The **Colorado Avalanche** have a unique tradition of playing "All the Small Things" by Blink-182 during the third period of home games. Fans sing along at the top of their lungs, creating a fun and energetic atmosphere that gets the crowd fired up.

The longest hockey stick ever used in a game was 6 feet long! It belonged to **Zdeno Chara,** who is also the tallest player ever, so it makes sense!

Some goalies think it's bad luck to have clean pads. They'll actually rub dirt on new equipment to make it look used!

In Indonesia, they have "Rice Paddy Hockey" - it's played on roller skates in empty rice fields during the dry season!

The "Curse of 1940" haunted the **New York Rangers** for over 50 years. After winning the Stanley Cup in 1940, they didn't win again until 1994. Some believed the curse was tied to the burning of the mortgage papers on Madison Square Garden using the Cup's flame!

Buffalo Sabres' player **Jeff Skinner** had a breakaway towards the net but forgot his stick behind. He tried dribbling the puck with his skates before losing it to the opposing team, which then scored on the other end. The visual of a stick-less player in full sprint is priceless.

Professional hockey players go through **80 to 120 sticks in a season** because they break during games or practice. Imagine needing that many spares!

Marty McSorley was known for his toughness, but in 1993, he made headlines for another reason. In Game 2 of the Stanley Cup Final, McSorley, playing for the Los Angeles Kings, was caught with an illegally curved stick. The **Montreal Canadiens** were awarded a power play and scored the game-tying goal, ultimately winning the game and the Cup.

Some players put special "shot blockers" on their skates - they're like plastic shields that protect the side of the skate from being hit by pucks.

The NHL's fastest skater competition is a fan favorite during the All-Star Weekend. Players like **Connor McDavid** and **Dylan Larkin** have dazzled crowds by racing around the rink at incredible speeds. Larkin set a new record in 2016 by completing a lap in 13.172 seconds.

One of the Greatest Comebacks in NHL History happened in 1982. The **Los Angeles Kings** were down 5-0 to the **Edmonton Oilers** in a playoff game, but they rallied to win 6-5 in overtime. The game became known as the "Miracle on Manchester," named after the street where the Kings' arena was located.

Vladimir Tarasenko, a star for the **St. Louis Blues**, helped lead his team to their first-ever Stanley Cup victory in 2019. The Blues had been the oldest franchise in the NHL without a championship, making their win an unforgettable moment for the team and its fans.

The Stanley Cup has a surprising rule: if a player damages the Cup, they have to pay for the repairs! Over the years, the Cup has had dents, scratches, and even been dropped into swimming pools by celebrating players.

Cameroon has a street hockey program where kids use banana leaves to make their own sticks! They're trying to build their first ice rink.

Patrick Roy, considered one of the greatest goalies in hockey history, is known for popularizing the "butterfly" style of goaltending. This technique involves dropping to the knees with pads flat to the ice, covering the lower part of the net. Today, nearly all goalies use this method, thanks to Roy.

In Japan, some hockey teams play music during the game - not just during breaks! They say it helps them stay energized.

Edmonton's **Wayne Gretzky** statue stands outside Rogers Place, honoring the greatest hockey player of all time. The statue shows Gretzky holding the Stanley Cup above his head, a reminder of the four championships he brought to the city during his career.

The longest undefeated streak in NHL history belongs to the **Philadelphia Flyers.** In the 1979-80 season, they went an incredible 35 games without losing, a record that still stands today.

Many players think using new laces in playoff games is bad luck. They'll use the same old laces even if they're almost broken!

Joe Thornton, known as "Jumbo Joe," is one of the NHL's greatest playmakers. He's tall—6'4"—and earned his nickname from his size and his hometown of St. Thomas, Ontario, which is known for its famous elephant, Jumbo. Thornton played over 1,700 NHL games and retired as the sixth-highest player for games played in league history.

The **Reading Royals** in Pennsylvania have a "Science of Hockey Night" where they demonstrate physics experiments using hockey equipment during intermissions!

◆

Evgeni Malkin, a star for the **Pittsburgh Penguins**, is known for his powerful skating and lethal shot. He's won multiple Stanley Cups alongside **Sidney Crosby**, and together they've formed one of the NHL's most dangerous one-two punches for over a decade.

◆

In the 2002 Winter Olympics, the Canadian women's hockey team made history by defeating the United States to win their first-ever Olympic gold medal in women's hockey. The rivalry between these two teams has since become one of the fiercest in sports.

◆

Connor Bedard, the young Canadian hockey phenom, became the first player in WHL history to be granted exceptional player status at the age of 15, meaning he could play in the league at a younger age than usual. His outstanding skills have earned him comparisons to **Sidney Crosby** and **Connor McDavid**.

Hockey players are known for their toughness, and **Duncan Keith** proved this in the 2010 playoffs when he lost seven teeth after being hit in the face with a puck. Keith continued to play and helped lead the **Chicago Blackhawks** to the Stanley Cup that year!

The Quebec Pee-Wee Tournament is the biggest youth hockey tournament in the world. Over 2,300 players compete each year!

The first hockey skates were just regular winter boots with blades strapped to them. Now they're specially designed with ankle support that lets players lean forward while skating - they're tilted about 15 degrees forward compared to normal shoes!

The **Ottawa Senators** were one of the most successful teams in the early days of the NHL, winning 11 Stanley Cups between 1920 and 1927. Although the team folded in 1934, a new version of the Senators was re-established in 1992 and has been competing in the NHL ever since.

Gordie Howe played professional hockey into his 50s, an age when most players have long retired. He even played alongside his two sons, Mark and Marty Howe, in the World Hockey Association (WHA), making him one of the few players to skate on the same team as his children.

Some players won't say the word "shutout" during a game where their team hasn't been scored on yet. They think saying it will jinx it!

The newest expansion team in the NHL currently is the **Utah Hockey Club**. Their home stadium is The Delta Center in Salt Lake City, Utah. Did you know the new team has already set a record? When their tickets went on sale, they sold over 6,000 deposits in just two hours! That's faster than most teams, showing how excited fans in Utah are for their first NHL team. Plus, their home games are played at the Delta Center, a venue with a cool history—it was part of the 2002 Winter Olympics! Utah's hockey scene is growing fast, and it's now one of the quirkiest new homes for ice hockey in the desert.

Anze Kopitar became the first Slovenian player to ever win the Stanley Cup. As captain of the **Los Angeles Kings**, Kopitar led his team to championships in 2012 and 2014. He is also considered one of the best defensive forwards in the league.

In a bizarre twist, a fan fell into the penalty box with **Tie Domi**, a tough guy known for his brawls. Chaos ensued, but Domi managed to keep his cool and later laughed about the encounter, which has since become legendary.

Jarome Iginla, a longtime captain of the **Calgary Flames**, was known for his leadership, scoring ability, and toughness. Iginla became the first Black player in NHL history to score 500 goals and was inducted into the Hockey Hall of Fame in 2020.

The Swedish Women's Hockey League (SDHL) has a team that travels by boat to some of their games because they're located on an island!

Hockey games can last a long time in overtime. In the 2020 playoffs, the **Tampa Bay Lightning** and **Columbus Blue Jackets** played a marathon game that lasted 150 minutes and 27 seconds, going into five overtimes! The game was so long that some players reportedly ate pizza between periods to stay energized.

The first hockey pucks were often made from frozen cow dung! You have to use what's available, right? Thankfully, today's pucks are made from vulcanized rubber, and they're frozen before games to reduce bouncing on the ice.

Valeri Kharlamov, a legendary Soviet Union hockey player, is considered one of the greatest players never to play in the NHL. His speed and skill dazzled in international tournaments, and he became famous for his performance during the 1972 Summit Series between Canada and the Soviet Union.

Braden Holtby, goalie for the **Washington Capitals**, made one of the most famous saves in Stanley Cup Final history in 2018. Known simply as "The Save," Holtby stopped a shot with his stick in Game 2, preserving the Capitals' lead and helping them win their first-ever championship.

The first all-girls hockey team in Kuwait started in 2017, and now they have enough players for a whole league!

The Broad Street Bullies was the nickname for the **Philadelphia Flyers** of the 1970s, who were known for their tough, physical style of play. They won back-to-back Stanley Cups in 1974 and 1975 by intimidating opponents and playing relentless hockey.

The first indoor hockey game in Antarctica was played in 2017. The players had to build the rink inside a research station!

Ken Dryden, the Hall of Fame goalie for the **Montreal Canadiens**, had a unique career. He won six Stanley Cups in only seven full NHL seasons, and what's even more amazing is that Dryden retired at just 31 years old to pursue a career in law and politics.

The fastest hat trick (three goals in one game by the same player) was scored in just 21 seconds by **Bill Mosienko** in 1952!

In the 2014 Sochi Olympics, the Canadian men's hockey team dominated the competition, allowing only three goals in six games to win the gold medal. Their defensive performance is still considered one of the best in international hockey history.

The Stanley Cup has been lost more than once! In 1905, members of the **Ottawa Senators** accidentally kicked the Cup into the Rideau Canal while celebrating. Luckily, it was recovered the next day, and the celebrations continued.

Teemu Selanne, known as the "Finnish Flash," scored 76 goals in his rookie season with the **Winnipeg Jets** in 1992-93, setting an NHL record that still stands today. In fact, no one has even come close to breaking the record! Selanne was known for his speed and goal-scoring ability throughout his Hall of Fame career.

Many players think it's bad luck to use a stick that scored three goals in one game (a hat trick). They'll retire that stick and never use it again!

Bobby Hull, known as "The Golden Jet," was famous for his blistering slapshot, which was once clocked at over 118 miles per hour! Hull's powerful shot revolutionized the way players approached shooting, making him one of the most feared goal-scorers of his era. His slapshot was so fast and powerful that it could dent boards!

The **Toronto Maple Leafs** last won the Stanley Cup in 1967, making them the team with the longest championship drought in NHL history. Despite the long wait, the Leafs remain one of the most popular and historic franchises in the league.

Mario Lemieux, known as "Super Mario," made an incredible comeback in 2000 after battling Hodgkin's lymphoma, a form of cancer. He returned to the NHL and scored a goal on his first shot in his first game back. Lemieux's resilience inspired fans around the world and cemented his legacy as one of the greatest players ever. Lemieux led the **Pittsburgh Penguins** to two Stanley Cup titles and won multiple scoring titles.

Some teams won't wash their jerseys during winning streaks. The locker room gets pretty stinky!

Peter Forsberg, one of the most talented players of his era, was known for his physical style of play and remarkable vision. He won two Stanley Cups with the **Colorado Avalanche** and is remembered for his iconic shootout goal in the 1994 Olympic gold medal game for Sweden. This was Sweden's first Olympic win and his goal is remembered as the "Gold Medal Goal"!

There's a hockey team in Australia called the **Sydney Ice Dogs**. They play during the Australian winter - which is summer in North America!

In the 1999 Stanley Cup Final, **Brett Hull**'s controversial goal in triple overtime gave the **Dallas Stars** their first championship. Hull's skate appeared to be in the crease, which was illegal at the time, but the goal stood, and the Stars claimed the Cup.

In 1976, **Darryl Sittler** of the **Toronto Maple Leafs** set an NHL record by scoring 10 points in a single game. Sittler recorded six goals and four assists against the Boston Bruins, a feat that remains unmatched in the NHL to this day.

The Jack Adams Award is given to the NHL's best coach each year. Legendary coaches like **Scotty Bowman** and **Joel Quenneville** have won the award multiple times, thanks to their ability to lead their teams to greatness.

Mark Howe, son of the legendary **Gordie Howe**, was a Hall of Fame defenseman in his own right. He had a long career in both the WHA and NHL, playing over 1,300 professional games and making a name for himself with his smooth skating and excellent defensive play.

Nicklas Lidstrom, one of the NHL's greatest players, accidentally scored on his own team during a game. The opposing team stood in stunned silence before celebrating the unintentional gift.

Tuukka Rask, the longtime goalie for the **Boston Bruins**, won the Vezina Trophy as the league's top goalie in 2014. Known for his calm demeanor and quick reflexes, Rask helped the Bruins win the Stanley Cup in 2011.

Some goalies refuse to have their picture taken during warmups. They think the camera will steal their good luck!

Bill Masterton tragically passed away after an on-ice accident in 1968, and the Bill Masterton Trophy was created in his honor. This award is given to the player who best exemplifies perseverance, sportsmanship, and dedication to hockey each season.

The triple gold club is an exclusive group of players who have won a Stanley Cup, an Olympic gold medal, and a World Championship. Only a select few, like **Sidney Crosby** and **Nicklas Lidström**, have achieved this rare hockey trifecta, showcasing their dominance at every level of the game.

The first-ever NWHL (National Women's Hockey League) game took place on October 11, 2015, between the **Buffalo Beauts** and the **Boston Pride**. The Pride won 4-1, and this game marked the start of a new era in professional women's hockey.

In 2016, the Boston Pride became the first team to win the Isobel Cup, the championship trophy of the NWHL. The Cup is named after **Lady Isobel Gathorne-Hardy**, the daughter of **Lord Stanley**, who was one of the earliest female hockey players.

Some players think it's bad luck to step on the lines painted on the ice when they're skating to the bench!

Kendall Coyne Schofield, one of the fastest skaters in the world, made history at the 2019 NHL All-Star Skills Competition. She was the first woman to compete in the event, blazing around the rink in the fastest skater competition and inspiring young players everywhere.

The Stanley Cup is the oldest trophy in North American sports. It was first awarded in 1893 - that's over 130 years ago!

Hilary Knight, a superstar in women's hockey, has represented the United States at multiple Olympic Games, winning gold in 2018. Knight is also one of the all-time leading scorers in women's international hockey and is currently the captain of the PWHL (Professional Women's Hockey League) team the **Boston Fleet**. With multiple Olympic medals and World Championships, she's a vocal advocate for equal opportunities for women in hockey. She's so accurate with the puck that she can shoot a quarter off the top of a water bottle!

In 1936, the first artificial ice rink in Europe was built inside a train! It was in Switzerland, and people could skate while traveling through the Alps.

◆

Paul Kariya once scored a goal after being knocked unconscious in a Stanley Cup Final game! (Don't worry - today we know better about concussion safety.)

In Nepal, they practice hockey at the highest rink in the world - it's more than 11,000 feet above sea level!

Marie-Philip Poulin, captain of the Canadian national team and captain of the PWHL team **Montreal Victoire**, has earned the nickname "Captain Clutch" because of her ability to score big goals in critical moments. She has scored the game-winning goal in two Olympic gold medal games, cementing her status as a hockey hero.

Pro players often have tiny marks or designs carved into their blade holders so equipment managers know whose skates are whose - with 23 players on a team, that's a lot of skates to keep track of!

◆

In 1974, the **Washington Capitals** set a record for the worst season ever, winning only 8 games out of 80! Don't worry - they got much better and won the Stanley Cup in 2018.

Digit Murphy coached the first professional women's hockey team in China and taught all her players to speak both English and Mandarin!

In 2020, the **Minnesota Whitecaps** and **Metropolitan Riveters** played the first-ever outdoor game in women's professional hockey. The game was part of the Hockey Day Minnesota celebration and helped shine a spotlight on the growing popularity of women's hockey.

A hockey player named **Taro Tsujimoto** was drafted by the Buffalo Sabres in 1974. The funny part? He didn't exist! The team's general manager made him up as a joke.

Hayley Wickenheiser is considered one of the greatest female hockey players of all time. She played for Team Canada in six Olympic Games, winning four gold medals and one silver. She was also the first woman to play full-time professional men's hockey in a position other than goalie! After her playing career, Wickenheiser became a doctor and now works with the **Toronto Maple Leafs** as an assistant director of player development.

Some players think it's bad luck to call their moms before a big game. (But good luck to call after!)

In Colombia, they have a hockey program where kids earn ice time by doing well in school!

The Stanley Cup has been used as a cereal bowl, a flower pot, and even a baptismal font! Players get to spend one day with it when their team wins.

Amanda Kessel, sister of NHL player **Phil Kessel**, has been a standout player for Team USA. She represented the USA team at seven World Championships and three Olympic Games. Known for her speed and scoring touch, Amanda helped Team USA win gold at the 2018 Winter Olympics. She has also played a pivotal role in the formation of the Professional Women's Hockey League (PWHL). Her advocacy for women's professional hockey has inspired many young girls to pursue their dreams of playing the game at the highest level!

The puck can travel so fast that TV cameras sometimes lose track of it. That's why they used to put a glowing effect on the puck for TV games!

The youngest player to ever score in the NHL was **Bep Guidolin**, who was just 16 years and 11 months old when he scored his first goal for the **Boston Bruins** in 1942. He was brought onto the team due to the holes in the roster left by players leaving to fight in World War II.

There's a hockey team in India that practices on a frozen lake in the Himalayas! The lake only freezes for a few weeks each year.

Rebecca Johnston has been a leader for Team Canada for many years, winning multiple gold medals in international play. Her incredible skill and leadership have made her one of the top players in women's hockey and a key figure for the Calgary Inferno before the team disbanded.

In Sweden, there's a hockey team called **Leksands IF** that has a lucky pig as their mascot. Fans throw plush pigs onto the ice for good luck!

Madison Packer, a star forward for the PWHL's **New York Sirens**, has been a leading scorer and a strong advocate for LGBTQ+ inclusion in hockey. Packer's leadership on and off the ice has made her a fan favorite and an important voice for diversity in the sport.

Patrick Roy used to do ballet in the off-season to improve his flexibility as a goalie. Many players take dance classes to help with skating!

The NWHL's creation helped inspire the formation of other women's hockey leagues around the world, including the Swedish Women's Hockey League (SDHL) and the Russian Women's Hockey League (ZhHL). These leagues have provided even more opportunities for women to play professionally.

◆

Bobby Hull shot the puck so hard that he once split a puck in half during a game!

◆

Brianna Decker, an American forward, has won multiple gold medals with Team USA and is one of the top scorers in women's hockey history. She finished her USA career with 81 goals and 170 points in 147 games! Decker has also played in the Premier Hockey Federation (PHF), helping to grow the league with her skill and leadership.

◆

The heaviest NHL player ever was **Dustin Byfuglien**, who weighed 265 pounds. The lightest was **Roy "Shrimp" Worters** at just 135 pounds!

Manon Rhéaume, the first woman to play in an NHL game, has been a huge supporter of women's hockey. A goalie, she signed a contract with the **Tampa Bay Lightning** in 1992 and appeared in preseason games in both 1992 and 1993. Her trailblazing career has inspired countless girls to pursue their dreams of playing professional hockey.

Many teams won't let black cats anywhere near their arena. This is a pretty common superstition in lots of sports!

The Finnish word for hockey stick is "jääkiekkomaila" - try saying that three times fast!

Sarah Nurse made history at the 2022 Winter Olympics, becoming the first Black woman to win a gold medal in hockey. Nurse set an Olympic record for points in a single women's tournament and continues to inspire young players with her success on the international stage. She is currently a star player for the **Toronto Sceptres** in the PWHL.

Hockey players can be penalized for not having their jersey tucked in! It's called the "Untucked Jersey Rule."

Mario Lemieux once scored five goals in five different ways in one game: even strength, power play, short-handed, penalty shot, and empty net. Nobody has done this since!

◆

Shannon Szabados is a two-time Olympic gold medalist for Team Canada in 2010 and 2014. On December 27, 2015, Szabados became the first woman goaltender to record a shutout in a men's professional hockey league, in a 33-save, 3–0 win for the Columbus Cottonmouths over the Huntsville Havoc. In December 2020, she announced the publication of a children's book written and illustrated by her, titled *Every Bunny Loves to Play*. Truly, a woman of many talents!

The Great **Gretzky** scored so many goals that if you took away all his goals, he'd still be the NHL's all-time points leader just from his assists!

◆

Some players eat the exact same meal before every game for good luck. **Patrick Roy** always ate spaghetti!

◆

In 2023, the Professional Women's Hockey League (PWHL) was established, uniting the best female hockey players in North America and aiming to create a sustainable league for women's professional hockey. This league seeks to provide greater opportunities and visibility for female athletes. The league currently consists of six teams, three each from Canada and the USA.

◆

In 1945, goalie **Steve Buzinski** was nicknamed "The Headless Horseman" because he often ducked when players shot the puck at him!

In Finland, many outdoor rinks are lit up at night so kids can play hockey under the Northern Lights!

The PWHL Draft allows teams to select the top talents from universities and international leagues, helping to foster new generations of female players. The inaugural draft in 2023 featured some of the best young players, highlighting the depth of talent in women's hockey.

Hockey players can burn up to 1,800 calories in a single game. That's like eating 15 bananas!

Tessa Bonhomme is an Olympic gold medalist for Team Canada in 2010 who has become a professional hockey reporter for The Sports Network (TSN). What's more, she's become an actress and appeared on such popular TV shows as "Man Seeking Woman," "Goon: Last of the Enforcers," "Letterkenny," and "Shoresy." What a talented person!

In the 2022 Olympics, Team USA Women defeated Team Canada in a thrilling shootout to win the gold medal. The match featured spectacular plays from stars like **Hilary Knight** and **Amanda Kessel**, showcasing the high level of skill and competitiveness in women's hockey.

The temperature of a hockey rink is usually kept at around 16°F (-9°C). That's cold enough to keep popsicles frozen!

The NHL Foundation has pledged support for the PWHL, providing resources to help develop women's hockey at all levels. This partnership aims to create a more equitable environment for female players and encourage growth within the sport.

Los Angeles Kings' captain **Dustin Brown** accidentally tried drinking from an upside-down water bottle during a game. Realizing his mistake, he played it cool as if nothing happened.

Some players think it's good luck to be the last one off the ice after warm-ups. Sometimes two players will wait each other out for several minutes!

The PWHL's social media presence has grown rapidly, allowing fans to connect with their favorite players and teams. The league shares highlights, behind-the-scenes content, and player interviews, helping to build excitement around women's hockey.

Some players tape their sticks the exact same way before every game for good luck. If they play badly, they might change their taping pattern!

In 2022, the **Colorado Avalanche** won their third Stanley Cup after defeating the **Tampa Bay Lightning** in a hard-fought six-game series. Led by superstar **Nathan MacKinnon** and captain **Gabriel Landeskog,** the Avalanche played an aggressive, fast-paced style that kept fans on the edge of their seats.

The Finnish women's national team has a player named **Noora Räty** who once played in a men's professional league! She was the first woman to do this in Finland.

In 2020, **Connor McDavid**, captain of the **Edmonton Oilers**, became the first player to record 100 points in a season during a 56-game schedule. His speed, vision, and playmaking ability have earned him a reputation as one of the most electrifying players in hockey today.

Jarome Iginla, a legendary power forward, is one of the most beloved players in NHL history. Iginla, who captained the **Calgary Flames**, became the first Black captain in NHL history and was known for his scoring ability, leadership, and community involvement.

Carey Price, goaltender for the **Montreal Canadiens**, became an inspiration in 2021 when he led his team to the Stanley Cup Finals despite long odds. His calm demeanor and incredible reflexes earned him the Conn

Smythe Trophy for playoff MVP and solidified his legacy as one of the best goalies of his generation.

Phil Esposito played a pivotal role in the historic 1972 Summit Series, an eight-game series between Canada and the Soviet Union. Esposito's leadership and scoring ability helped lead Canada to a dramatic victory, and his emotional post-game speech after a loss in Game 4 galvanized the team and the nation.

The Harvard women's hockey team has a tradition where they write inspiring messages on paper stars and stick them to their locker room ceiling.

In 2021, **Alex Ovechkin** of the **Washington Capitals** surpassed **Marcel Dionne** on the all-time goal-scoring list. Ovechkin is regarded as one of the greatest goal scorers in NHL history, known for his booming slapshot and his famous spot on the power play.

Team Japan's women's hockey team is nicknamed "Smile Japan" because they always try to play with joy, no matter the score!

The **Detroit Red Wings** hold the record for the longest consecutive playoff appearance streak in NHL history, qualifying for the playoffs for 25 straight seasons from 1991 to 2016. This era included several Stanley Cup victories and featured stars like **Steve Yzerman**, **Nicklas Lidström**, and **Sergei Fedorov**.

The Swiss league has a team that plays in a 110-year-old castle! The rink is built in the castle's courtyard.

Many players tap their stick on the ice exactly three times before face-offs for luck.

Zdeno Chára, at 6 feet 9 inches(!), is the tallest player in NHL history. The towering defenseman played for the

Boston Bruins and captained the team to a Stanley Cup in 2011. Despite his size, Chára is known for his skating ability and powerful shot. His nickname is "Big Z."

Maurice "Rocket" Richard once played with a broken ankle - and still scored 5 goals! His coach found out after the game and wasn't happy.

Ray Bourque, one of the greatest defensemen in NHL history, spent 21 seasons with the **Boston Bruins** before joining the **Colorado Avalanche** late in his career. In 2001, Bourque finally won his first Stanley Cup, a heart-warming moment as his teammates handed him the Cup first to celebrate his illustrious career.

Vladislav Tretiak, a legendary Soviet goaltender, was one of the greatest netminders in hockey history. His dominance during the 1970s made him an international star, and although he never played in the NHL, he is still revered worldwide for his contributions to the game.

Some Finnish players eat reindeer meat before games for extra energy. It's a traditional food in Finland!

Martin Brodeur, widely regarded as one of the best goaltenders in NHL history, holds the record for most wins by a goalie with 691. He spent the majority of his career with the **New Jersey Devils**, leading them to three Stanley Cup victories and winning four Vezina Trophies.

Fun fact: **Martin Brodeur** used to drink water only from one specific water bottle. If someone moved it, he'd search until he found it!

The Norwegian women's team has identical twins who play defense together. Opponents say it's like trying to score against the same player twice!

The Golden Goal by **Sidney Crosby** during the 2010 Vancouver Winter Olympics is one of the most iconic moments in Canadian sports history. His overtime goal against the USA secured the gold medal for Canada, sending the entire nation into celebration.

Johnny Bower, nicknamed "The China Wall," was a legendary goalie for the **Toronto Maple Leafs** in the 1960s. Known for his acrobatic style and fearless play, Bower helped lead the Leafs to multiple Stanley Cup victories and is remembered as one of the toughest goalies to ever play the game. Funny fact: He used to tell ghost stories to his teammates before playoff games to help them relax!

A fascinating example of a chaotic puck moment occurred during a **Minnesota Wild** vs. **Tampa Bay Lightning** game, involving not one but **two pucks on the ice simultaneously**. In the confusion, **Marco Rossi** of the Wild scored with the wrong puck, leaving both players and fans bewildered. This bizarre incident led to a debate about how such a mishap could happen in professional hockey, as it's rare for extra pucks to make their way onto the ice during play.

In Ecuador, they started a roller hockey league that plays in the mountains - they're slowly transitioning to ice hockey as they build rinks!

"The Original Six" refers to the six teams that made up the NHL from 1942 to 1967: the **Boston Bruins, Chicago Blackhawks, Detroit Red Wings, Montreal Canadiens, New York Rangers,** and **Toronto Maple Leafs**. This era is often seen as the foundation of modern hockey history.

The **Vegas Golden Knights** have a real knight who rides onto the ice on a hoverboard before games! He even has a sword fight with the opposing team's mascot.

The Women's Ice Hockey World Championships are held annually and feature the best teams from around the world. Since its inception in 1990, the event has helped grow women's hockey, providing a platform for the top female players to showcase their skills on an international stage.

The **Glasgow Clan** in Scotland sometimes plays games where fans wear kilts and bring bagpipes to play during breaks!

In 2008, **Detroit Red Wings** defenseman **Nicklas Lidström** became the first European-born captain to win the Stanley Cup. Lidström, known for his calm demeanor and elite defensive skills, was one of the best blue-liners to ever play the game.

The KHL (Kontinental Hockey League) in Russia has a team that plays in China! It's called the **Kunlun Red Star.**

T.J. Oshie became an American hero during the 2014 Sochi Olympics when he scored four shootout goals in a single game to help Team USA defeat Russia in the group stage. Oshie's clutch performance under pressure made him an instant star back home.

The Korean women's ice hockey team made history at the 2018 Olympics when North and South Korea played together as one team!

The **Boston Bruins**' "Spoked-B" logo is one of the most recognizable symbols in hockey. The Bruins, one of the Original Six teams, have won multiple Stanley Cups, with legends like **Bobby Orr**, **Phil Esposito**, and **Ray Bourque** leading the way over the years.

Some players think it's bad luck to use brand-new equipment in important games. They'll break in new stuff during practice only.

The **Indy Fuel** have a mascot named **Nitro** who drives a mini Zamboni and shoots flames from its exhaust pipes!

The first hockey game broadcast on radio was in 1923. The announcer had to yell really loud because microphones weren't very good back then!

Kim St-Pierre is a three-time Olympic gold medalist and one of the most successful female goaltenders in hockey history. She played for Team Canada and set numerous records, including the most wins in women's Olympic hockey history.

In 2019, **Ryan O'Reilly** led the **St. Louis Blues** to their first Stanley Cup in franchise history. After being in last place halfway through the season, the Blues went on an incredible run, with O'Reilly winning the Conn Smythe Trophy as playoff MVP.

Caroline Ouellette, a four-time Olympic gold medalist with Team Canada, is one of the most decorated female hockey players in history. Known for her leadership and scoring ability, Ouellette has inspired countless young girls to pursue hockey.

Some arenas have special "Kid Captain" programs where a young fan gets to help lead the team onto the ice before the game.

In 1996, the **Florida Panthers** made it to the Stanley Cup Final in just their third season of existence. The "Rat Trick" tradition for the team started when Scott Mellanby killed a rat in the locker room and then scored two goals that night. Fans began throwing rubber rats onto the ice after every goal, creating the famous "Rat Trick" celebration that became a defining moment of that playoff run.

◆

Olympic hockey player **Renata Fast** can skate backward faster than most people can run forward!

◆

In Malaysia, they have "Midnight Hockey" leagues because it's too hot to play during the day, even inside the rink!

◆

Many teams have lucky lockers in their locker room. Young players often get stuck with the "unlucky" spots.

Julie Chu, one of the most decorated American women's hockey players, has been a trailblazer in the sport. With five World Championship golds and four Olympic medals, she played for Team USA for over a decade. Chu's leadership both on and off the ice has inspired countless young girls to pursue their hockey dreams.

The **Vancouver Canucks**' mascot is a killer whale named **Fin** who sometimes ziplines across the arena before games!

The **Tampa Bay Lightning** became back-to-back Stanley Cup champions in 2020 and 2021. Known for their incredible depth, they were led by stars like **Nikita Kucherov**, **Steven Stamkos**, and goalie **Andrei Vasilevskiy**, who was awarded the Conn Smythe Trophy in 2021 for his outstanding playoff performance. Known as "The Big Cat," Vasilevskiy's poise under pressure helped Tampa Bay capture back-to-back Stanley Cups.

"Jagrmania" swept the NHL in the 1990s, thanks to the electrifying play of **Jaromir Jagr**. Known for his incredible mullet, his powerful skating, and his unmatched scoring ability, Jagr went on to play until he was 45 years old, becoming the second-highest point scorer in NHL history behind **Wayne Gretzky**.

The **New York Rangers** once had a player who was afraid of flying. So he took the train to away games while his teammates flew!

In China, some schools now have hockey as part of gym class! They're trying to get more kids interested in the sport before the 2026 Winter Olympics.

The **Washington Capitals** finally won their first Stanley Cup in 2018, led by **Alex Ovechkin**, who was named Conn Smythe Trophy winner as playoff MVP. Ovechkin, known for his booming shot and physical play, celebrated by diving into a fountain with teammates, creating one of the most fun post-championship celebrations in recent memory!

Hockey player **Craig MacTavish** was the last NHL player to play without a helmet - he was allowed because he started before they were required!

In the 2002 Winter Olympics, **Jarome Iginla** assisted on **Mario Lemieux**'s famous no-look, through-the-legs pass that led to **Joe Sakic**'s goal. That play helped Canada win its first men's hockey gold medal in 50 years, with Iginla becoming the first Black athlete to win Olympic gold in hockey.

The **Manitoba Moose** have a tradition where players can only grow mustaches (no beards) during their playoff runs.

The **Vegas Golden Knights**, an expansion team in 2017, shocked the world by making it to the Stanley Cup Finals in their very first season. Led by coach **Gerard Gallant** and stars like goalie **Marc-André Fleury**, the Knights' Cinderella story captivated hockey fans worldwide.

Hockey player **Brandon Prust** used to write jokes on his stick tape to make his linemates laugh during face-offs.

Ken Dryden, the **Montreal Canadiens** goalie of the 1970s, had an unusual path to the NHL. He was a law student and played only six regular-season games before leading the Canadiens to the Stanley Cup in 1971. His book, The Game, is one of the most famous books about hockey ever written.

Some players think it's bad luck to step on the blue lines during warmups. They'll jump over every single one!

The **Calgary Flames** have a unique mascot, **Harvey the Hound**, who became famous when **Edmonton Oilers** coach **Craig MacTavish** ripped out his tongue during a heated game in 2003. Harvey's tongue-ripping incident remains one of the funniest and most bizarre moments in hockey mascot history!

In Burma (Myanmar), they have a hockey academy where kids learn both hockey AND English by watching game broadcasts!

Jocelyne Lamoureux-Davidson pulled off an incredible shootout goal in the 2018 Winter Olympics to give Team USA a gold medal victory over Canada in women's hockey. Her dazzling move, known as "Oops, I Did It Again," cemented her place in Olympic history.

In 2010, Team USA's **Zach Parise** scored a dramatic last-minute goal to tie the Olympic gold medal game against Canada. While Canada eventually won in overtime on **Sidney Crosby**'s "Golden Goal," Parise's clutch performance made that final one of the greatest games in Olympic hockey history.

◆

During the 2020 COVID pandemic, when teams couldn't meet in person, they had to practice and hold meetings over video calls, making it feel like a hockey training session on a computer screen!

◆

Elvis Merzļikins, the Latvian goalie for the **Columbus Blue Jackets**, made headlines in 2021 when he dedicated his shutout victory to fellow goalie and close friend **Matīss Kivlenieks**, who tragically passed away in a fireworks accident. Merzļikins' emotional tribute showed the close-knit bond between teammates.

The **Carolina Hurricanes** became famous for their post-game "Storm Surge" celebrations, where players would perform choreographed routines with fans after home victories. The celebrations, led by captain **Justin Williams**, became a viral sensation and made the team one of the most entertaining to watch.

The Jamaican Olympic Ice Hockey Federation started in 2011 and hopes to be "Cool Runnings on Ice!" They practice in Canada because Jamaica has no ice rinks.

Angela James, often called the "Wayne Gretzky of women's hockey," was one of the first women inducted into the Hockey Hall of Fame in 2010. She was a dominant scorer for Team Canada in the 1980s and 1990s, and her induction marked a milestone in the recognition of women's hockey achievements.

Many goalies mark their crease with tiny scratches that only they can see - they think it helps them know where they are in the net.

The **Montreal Canadiens** have a tradition where kids throw toast on the ice when a player scores three goals. It's called a "toast trick" instead of a hat trick!

The KHL (Kontinental Hockey League) is the top professional league in Russia and is often seen as the second-best hockey league in the world after the NHL. It attracts top international talent and provides a high level of competition, especially from teams like **CSKA Moscow** and **SKA Saint Petersburg**.

The **Idaho Steelheads** have "Potato Night" where they use a potato as a puck for one ceremonial face-off!

Chris Pronger, a towering defenseman known for his toughness and skill, won both the Hart Trophy and Norris Trophy in 2000, a rare feat for a defenseman. He led the **St. Louis Blues** and later the **Anaheim Ducks** to a Stanley Cup in 2007. He was so tall (6'6") that he had to duck to avoid hitting his head on many locker room doorways!

Tim Horton, best known for the coffee chain that bears his name, was also a Hall of Fame defenseman for the **Toronto Maple Leafs**. He was a four-time Stanley Cup champion and is remembered as one of the toughest and most reliable players of his era.

Some hockey players put tiny bells in their gloves during practice to help them know if they're gripping their stick too tight!

In 2022, the **New York Rangers** made a deep playoff run, inspired by their star goalie **Igor Shesterkin**, who won the Vezina Trophy as the NHL's top goaltender. Shesterkin's clutch saves and composure under pressure made him one of the most exciting players in the league.

Jayna Hefford, one of the most decorated players in women's hockey, won four Olympic gold medals with Team Canada. Known for her speed and offensive ability, Hefford became a key figure in the development of women's hockey in Canada and globally.

The Minnesota State High School Hockey Tournament is so popular that it sometimes gets higher TV ratings than NHL games!

The **Los Angeles Kings** won their first Stanley Cup in 2012 as an eighth seed, the lowest seed ever to win the Cup! Led by goalie **Jonathan Quick** and captain **Dustin Brown**, the Kings' remarkable playoff run is considered one of the greatest underdog stories in NHL history.

Lanny McDonald, known for his big red mustache and scoring ability, captained the **Calgary Flames** to their first and only Stanley Cup in 1989. McDonald's leadership and personality made him one of the most beloved figures in Flames history.

Some players think it's bad luck to say "good luck" - they say "bad luck" instead because they think it reverses the jinx!

Jari Kurri became the first Finnish player inducted into the Hockey Hall of Fame in 2001. A key player in the **Edmonton Oilers** dynasty of the 1980s, Kurri formed a dynamic duo with **Wayne Gretzky**, helping the team win five Stanley Cups.

Patrick Kane, one of the most skilled American-born players in NHL history, won the Hart Trophy in 2016 and helped lead the **Chicago Blackhawks** to three Stanley Cup championships. Kane's dazzling stickhandling and clutch performances have made him one of the most popular players in the league.

There's a team in Slovakia that plays in an outdoor arena with a roof but no walls - even in winter! The fans just bundle up really warm.

In the 1980s, **Paul Coffey** was known as one of the fastest skaters and top defensemen in the NHL. He scored 48 goals in a single season with the **Edmonton Oilers**, setting a record for defensemen that still stands today. Coffey's blistering speed and scoring made him an unforgettable part of the Oilers' dynasty years.

NHL player **Mats Zuccarello** learned to play hockey in Norway by practicing in his tiny basement. He would shoot pucks at washing machines!

NHL referees are known for their intense training and physical endurance, as they skate an average of five miles every game! They also memorize the rule book and make hundreds of split-second decisions during each game, making their job one of the toughest on the ice.

The Paris Hockey Club in France plays in a rink that has the Eiffel Tower painted on the ice. At night, the painting glows in the dark!

Natalie Spooner, a standout for Team Canada's women's hockey team, has not only won medals on the ice but has also competed on reality TV shows, showing off her strength and determination. Spooner's ability to balance hockey with other pursuits has inspired fans to pursue their dreams both on and off the ice. She continues to play, currently for the **Toronto Sceptres** in the PWHL, and runs a High Performance Hockey Academy for girls!

The 2022 Beijing Winter Olympics saw the debut of **Sarah Fillier** on Canada's women's hockey team, where she quickly made an impact with her scoring abilities. Fillier's strong performance helped her team secure gold, and she's now considered one of hockey's brightest young stars. She plays for the PWHL's **New York Sirens**.

The **Montreal Canadiens'** arena is built on top of an underground river. Sometimes during playoffs, fans say they can hear the water running for good luck!

The Switzerland women's national team has a tradition where they all braid their hair the same way before important games for good luck.

The **Mighty Ducks** of Anaheim, a team named after a Disney movie, joined the NHL in 1993. Surprisingly, they made it to the Stanley Cup Final in 2003, becoming one of the most unique teams in the league. Their early success helped build a new fan base for hockey in Southern California.

Erik Karlsson, one of the NHL's most dynamic defensemen, overcame a major injury to return to the league with the **San Jose Sharks**. Known for his smooth skating and playmaking ability, Karlsson is one of the few defensemen to lead his team in scoring.

In Romania, there's a hockey team that plays in a rink built inside an old salt mine, 400 feet underground!

Some NHL players paint their toenails team colors for luck - but they don't tell anyone about it!

The **New York Islanders** won four consecutive Stanley Cups from 1980 to 1983, a rare feat that showed their dominance. Led by stars like **Mike Bossy**, **Bryan Trottier**, and **Billy Smith**, the Islanders built one of hockey's greatest dynasties, winning 19 straight playoff series over that stretch.

Laura Stacey, a forward for Team Canada, is not only a hockey star but also the great-granddaughter of Hockey Hall of Famer **King Clancy**. Following in her family's footsteps, Stacey has represented Canada on the international stage, and now the **Montreal Victoire,** becoming an ambassador for women's hockey.

Owen Power, drafted first overall by the **Buffalo Sabres** in 2021, took an unusual route by playing an extra year of college hockey after being drafted. Power's decision showcased his commitment to developing his skills and preparing himself fully before joining the NHL.

The KHL's **Red Army** team, based in Moscow, was once the most dominant hockey club in the world. During the Cold War era, their players were part of a rigorous training program, and many of them also played for the Soviet national team, winning gold medals and world championships.

The **Edmonton Oilers** have a secret popcorn tradition - they make special orange and blue popcorn (team colors) for good luck before playoff games.

The 1972 Summit Series between Canada and the Soviet Union was a historic eight-game showdown that captured the world's attention. Canada narrowly won the series thanks to **Paul Henderson's** game-winning goal in the final minute of the last game, a moment still celebrated in Canadian hockey history.

Some players think it's bad luck to smile in team photos on game days. That's why they look so serious!

Mason McTavish, an up-and-coming young star, saved Team Canada from a heartbreaking loss in the 2022 IIHF World Junior Championship by making a last-second goal-line save. McTavish's defensive play turned into a golden opportunity, leading to Canada's eventual championship win in overtime. McTavish made his NHL debut with the **Anaheim Ducks** in 2021.

The Mexican national women's team started in 2012 and has grown so much that they now have youth programs in 27 states!

Cassie Campbell-Pascall, former captain of Team Canada's women's hockey team, became the first woman to do color commentary on Hockey Night in Canada, the longest-running sports TV show in the world! Campbell-Pascall's achievements on the ice and her work in broadcasting have paved the way for more women in the sport.

Cale Makar, a young defenseman for the **Colorado Avalanche**, is often compared to legends like **Bobby Orr**

because of his offensive skill and skating ability. Makar won the Calder Trophy as rookie of the year and helped the Avalanche win the Stanley Cup in 2022.

In Sweden, there's a tournament where girls and boys play on the same teams until they're teenagers. They say it makes everyone better players!

Hockey player **Georges Vézina** played 16 years without ever missing a game - even though he didn't know how to skate when he first started playing goalie! He was a legendary goaltender for the **Montreal Canadiens.** He now has a trophy, the Vezina Trophy, that is awarded in the NHL each year to the best goaltender!

◆

Pat LaFontaine, known for his sportsmanship and dedication, is one of only a few NHL players to be inducted into the Hockey Hall of Fame without winning a Stanley Cup. LaFontaine's positive attitude and love for the game made him one of the most respected players of his era.

The Flying V, a legendary play featured in "The Mighty Ducks" movies, may not work in a real NHL game, but it has inspired countless young players. The formation, where the team skates down the ice in a V shape, symbolizes teamwork and creativity.

Dustin Byfuglien, known for his powerful hits and big personality, played both forward and defense during his NHL career. Byfuglien's versatility and physical style of play made him a fan favorite, especially during his time with the **Winnipeg Jets**.

In South Africa, they have a hockey program where kids learn to skate using chairs with hockey sticks attached to them!

Ryan Miller is one of the winningest American-born goalies in NHL history and was a hero for Team USA during the 2010 Olympics. His goaltending performance helped the U.S. reach the gold medal game, which they narrowly lost to Canada in overtime.

Artemi Panarin, nicknamed "The Breadman," overcame a tough upbringing in Russia to become one of the NHL's most skilled forwards. Panarin's creative playmaking and high-scoring talent have made him a superstar with the **New York Rangers.**

The longest women's hockey game ever played lasted 170 minutes and 9 seconds in the NCAA Championship! It was even longer than some NHL playoff games.

Pavel Bure, also known as "The Russian Rocket," was one of the fastest and most explosive players in NHL history. Bure's breakaway speed and goal-scoring talent earned him two 60-goal seasons with the **Vancouver Canucks** and a place in the Hockey Hall of Fame.

Hockey player **Mike Green** used to paint his sticks neon green so his teammates could see them better during games!

Börje Salming is a legend in the NHL and in his home country of Sweden. He was a trailblazer in the NHL as one of the first Europeans in the league, spending 16 seasons with the **Toronto Maple Leafs** who retired his jersey number 21 in 2016. Salming became the first European-born and trained player inducted into the Hockey Hall of Fame in 1996. In 2017, the NHL named Salming one of the 100 Greatest Players in league history.

Thailand has a women's hockey team that practices in a shopping mall! The ice rink is right next to the food court.

The **Carolina Hurricanes** have a victory celebration where they pretend to go bowling - using a player as the ball and their teammates as pins!

Mikko Koivu is one of Finland's most respected hockey players, known for his leadership and two-way play. He became the first player in **Minnesota Wild** history to have his number retired, showing the impact he had on the team and fans.

Igor Larionov, known as "The Professor," was one of the smartest players of his era and a pioneer for Russian players in the NHL. Larionov helped the **Detroit Red Wings** win multiple Stanley Cups and was known for his playmaking ability and hockey IQ.

The University of Minnesota women's hockey team once won 62 games in a row! That's the longest winning streak in college hockey history.

◆

Johnny Gaudreau, known as "Johnny Hockey," defied the odds with his small size (5'9") to become an elite NHL scorer. Gaudreau's quickness and skill helped him become a fan favorite and an inspiration for smaller players aiming to reach the NHL. Sadly, Gaudreau passed away after he and his brother Matthew, also a hockey player, were struck by a drunk driver in 2024. The entire hockey world mourned his loss, as well as politicians like Canadian Prime Minister Justin Trudeau and the governors of Gaudreau's home state of New Jersey. Fellow American NHL player and U.S. National teammate **Cole Caulfield** announced he would be switching his jersey number to 13 to honor Gaudreau, saying he was an inspiration to him early in his career. All of this shows how close the hockey community is.

The **Sheffield Steelers** in England have a fan who has watched every home game for 30 years while knitting hockey scarves. She's made over 1,000!

Mark Messier is one of the most celebrated leaders in NHL history, famously guaranteeing a win in Game 6 of the 1994 Eastern Conference Finals and delivering with a hat trick. He led the **New York Rangers** to their first Stanley Cup in 54 years that season, solidifying his place as one of the game's greatest captains. He has an NHL award named after him that goes to the player demonstrating the highest leadership each season.

Jennifer Botterill scored the fastest goal in women's hockey history - just 8 seconds after the game started!

The **Ottawa Senators** were one of the original teams in the NHL, founded in 1883, and won multiple Stanley Cups in the early 20th century before the franchise folded. The team was re-established in 1992, bringing back a piece of Canadian hockey history to the nation's capital!

Mikko Rantanen is a rising star with the **Colorado Avalanche** known for his size, skill, and scoring touch. Alongside **Nathan MacKinnon**, Rantanen has helped turn the Avalanche into one of the most powerful teams in the league, playing a big role in their 2022 Stanley Cup win.

Sergei Fedorov was one of the NHL's first Russian superstars, joining the **Detroit Red Wings** in 1990 after defecting from the Soviet Union. Known for his speed and two-way play, Fedorov won three Stanley Cups with Detroit and helped open the door for other Russian players in the NHL. He was the first Russian player to win the Hart Trophy as the NHL's MVP in 1994.

Doug Gilmour was known for his gritty play and impressive scoring ability, particularly during his time with the **Toronto Maple Leafs**. His energetic style and performances under pressure in the playoffs earned him the nickname "Killer" and made him a hero in Toronto.

The NHL Draft Lottery can be a huge moment for rebuilding teams, as it determines which teams get the top picks. Winning the lottery has helped struggling teams draft future stars like **Connor McDavid, Auston Matthews,** and **Jack Hughes**, shaping the future of the league.

Joe Sakic, known for his wrist shot, was one of the most respected players on and off the ice. After his retirement, Sakic moved to a management role and helped build the **Colorado Avalanche** into a Stanley Cup-winning team in 2022 as their General Manager.

Chris Chelios played an incredible 26 seasons in the NHL, retiring at age 48, making him one of the oldest players in league history. His longevity and fierce style of play made him a legend in cities like Chicago and Detroit, where he won three Stanley Cups.

The **Winnipeg Jets'** "whiteout" is one of the most electrifying fan traditions in hockey. Fans fill the arena dressed in all white, creating an unforgettable, intimidating atmosphere during playoff games—a tradition that started in the 1980s and continues today!

The Russian women's hockey league is called the "ZhHL" and has teams that travel across 7 time zones to play each other!

Brett Hull famously scored the controversial goal that won the **Dallas Stars** the Stanley Cup in 1999. His foot was in the crease when he scored, which was technically against the rules at the time, but the goal stood and remains one of the most debated moments in NHL history.

Olympic gold medalist **Meghan Agosta** worked as a police officer while playing professional hockey. Her nickname was "The Hockey Cop!"

The **Tampa Bay Lightning**, also known as "the Bolts", won the Stanley Cup in both 2020 and 2021, becoming back-to-back champions and proving themselves as one of the most dominant teams of the era. Their consistency and skill have set a high standard for success in the modern NHL.

Patty Kazmaier was a standout college hockey player whose legacy lives on through the Patty Kazmaier Award, given annually to the top female college hockey player in the United States. Her passion and talent have inspired many young players aiming to play college hockey.

The **Chicago Blackhawks**' logo, featuring a Native American figure, is one of the most recognizable in sports. The team has worked with Native American communities to ensure respectful representation, showing the importance of dialogue in honoring culture in sports.

Some players on Team Slovakia practice their shooting by using glow-in-the-dark pucks at night! They say it helps them focus better.

John Tavares created a huge stir in 2018 when he left the New York Islanders to sign with his hometown team, the **Toronto Maple Leafs**. This homecoming was met with both joy and heartbreak, showing the deep connection fans feel toward players and teams. Tavares went on to become captain of the Maple Leafs and a consistently high-scorer.

The **New Jersey Devils**' "Trap" defense strategy was so effective in the 1990s that it led to the team winning multiple Stanley Cups. This defensive style slowed down games and frustrated opponents, and it left a lasting impact on how teams approach defense.

Grant Fuhr was one of the first Black players to become a star in the NHL, winning multiple Stanley Cups with the **Edmonton Oilers**. His agility and calm demeanor made him one of the best goalies of his time, helping break barriers in hockey.

The **New York Rangers**' "Garden Faithful" are some of the most passionate fans in hockey, filling Madison Square Garden with energy and excitement every game. The loyalty of Rangers fans has made the team's home games an unforgettable experience.

Vancouver's "Green Men", two fans in green spandex suits, became famous for their antics and cheers behind the opponents' penalty box during **Canucks** games. Their dedication and creativity showed how fans can become a big part of a team's spirit.

Willie O'Ree broke the NHL's color barrier in 1958, becoming the first Black player in the league. His courage and dedication paved the way for future generations of players from diverse backgrounds, and he continues to be a symbol of inclusivity in hockey.

Taylor Hall, the first overall pick in 2010, has played for multiple teams and is known for his speed and scoring ability. His career path has shown the unpredictable journey that many players experience in pursuit of their NHL dreams.

The Stanley Cup Parade in Montreal used to be so popular that it would shut down the city, with fans lining the streets to catch a glimpse of the players and the trophy. This tradition highlighted the deep connection between the **Canadiens** and their loyal fanbase.

The **Columbus Blue Jackets**' cannon is fired every time the team scores at home, creating a unique and thrilling experience for fans. The tradition adds a special touch to games and gets fans on their feet with every goal!

The Spanish Ice Hockey Federation has a program where they teach hockey and figure skating to kids with disabilities. They call it "Hockey Para Todos" (Hockey for Everyone)!

Nashville Predators fans have a tradition of throwing catfish onto the ice during playoff games, similar to Detroit's octopus-throwing tradition. The catfish toss has become a beloved symbol of Nashville's fun-loving fan culture.

New York Islanders legend **Mike Bossy** was one of the most natural goal scorers in NHL history, scoring 50 goals in nine consecutive seasons! His ability to find the back of the net made him a crucial part of the Islanders' dynasty in the early 1980s.

◆

The **Arizona Coyotes** once had a game delayed because a coyote (a real one!) wandered onto the ice during warm-ups.

Cammi Granato was one of the first women to be inducted into the Hockey Hall of Fame, recognized for her achievements and contributions to women's hockey. Her pioneering career helped raise the profile of women's hockey and paved the way for future stars.

The **Montreal Canadiens** once played with too many players celebrating a goal, so they got a penalty. But they were already winning by so much (9-1), they posed for a team photo while sitting in the penalty box!

The **Seattle Kraken**'s mascot, **Buoy**, is a friendly and colorful character who captures the spirit of Seattle's unique and quirky culture. Buoy's antics have quickly made him a beloved figure at Kraken games, adding fun to the team's atmosphere.

Auston Matthews, the **Toronto Maple Leafs**' star, made history as the first player from Arizona to be drafted first overall in the NHL. His success has helped grow hockey in non-traditional markets, showing young players from everywhere that hockey is for everyone!

The **New Jersey Devils**' "Hughes Brothers", **Jack** and **Luke**, have both been top NHL draft picks and are set to make a big impact on their team. As the first siblings to be drafted in the top 10 for the Devils, they've become a source of excitement for fans and a testament to the role of family in hockey development.

Martin St. Louis overcame his small stature—standing only 5'8"—to become a two-time Art Ross Trophy winner and a Stanley Cup champion with the **Tampa Bay Lightning**. Known for his relentless work ethic, St. Louis scored 1,033 points in his NHL career, proving that determination and heart can surpass any height disadvantage!

There's a team in New Zealand called the **Ice Fernz** (named after their national plant). They practice at 5 AM because that's when they can get ice time!

The "**Stastny Brothers**," **Peter**, **Anton**, and **Marian**, became hockey legends after defecting from Czechoslovakia to play in the NHL in the 1980s. Together, they totaled over 2,000 points, with Peter becoming one of the first European players to reach superstar status and pave the way for European talent in the league.

Connor Hellebuyck set a record for American goalies in 2020 by leading the league in wins and securing the Vezina Trophy. Known for his calm and unflappable demeanor in the net, Hellebuyck's skill and resilience have made him one of the best goalies of his generation.

In Singapore, they have "Tropical Ice Hockey" tournaments where the temperature outside is 90°F (32°C), but they're playing on ice!

Sidney Crosby scored his first NHL goal on October 8, 2005, against the **Boston Bruins**, setting the stage for a remarkable career. With over 500 career goals and 1,500 points, Crosby has solidified his place as one of hockey's greatest players and an inspiration to young athletes worldwide.

Hockey player **Bobby Ryan** once scored a goal using another player's stick after his broke! He grabbed it off the ice mid-play.

Auston Matthews became the first player in **Toronto Maple Leafs** history to score 60 goals in a season during 2021-22. His incredible scoring ability has made him one of the league's top players and a role model for the next generation of hockey stars.

Some teams in Russia have special heated benches for players because their rinks are so cold that regular benches would freeze!

Jonathan Quick, known for his acrobatic saves, led the **Los Angeles Kings** to two Stanley Cups in 2012 and

2014. With over 370 career wins, his perseverance and athleticism have set a standard for excellence in goaltending.

Guy Lafleur was known as "The Flower" and was famous for his speed and style on the ice. With 560 career goals and 1,353 points, Lafleur's electrifying play brought fans to their feet and established him as one of **Montreal Canadiens**' all-time legends.

Patrick Marleau broke **Gordie Howe**'s record for most games played, totaling 1,779 games by the end of his career in 2021. Known for his sportsmanship and dedication, Marleau's record showcases the longevity and resilience needed to succeed in the NHL.

The Ukrainian Hockey League has a rule that every team must have at least one girls' team too. They want to grow the sport for everyone!

The "Flying Frenchmen" was a nickname for the high-flying **Montreal Canadiens** teams in the 1910s and 1920s. Known for their speed and finesse, they dominated Canadian hockey, helping to build a fanbase that would grow into one of the most loyal in sports.

Modern hockey helmets can handle impacts of up to 100 times the force of gravity! That's why they have to be replaced after any big hit - the foam inside compresses to absorb the shock, but can only do this job properly once.

Milan Hejduk spent his entire 14-season NHL career with the **Colorado Avalanche**, scoring 375 goals. Known for his accurate shot and loyalty to his team, Hejduk's commitment left a lasting impact on Avalanche fans and the city of Denver.

Dustin Byfuglien was one of the most intimidating and versatile players, known for his powerful hits and unique ability to play both defense and forward. His physical style and 500 career points made him a fan favorite and a game-changer for the **Winnipeg Jets**.

Rod Brind'Amour, known for his work ethic and leadership, captained the **Carolina Hurricanes** to their first Stanley Cup in 2006. His legacy lives on as the team's head coach, where he continues to inspire players to give their best every game.

The **Minnesota Wild** once had a "State of Hockey" game where every player wore jerseys with their hometown written on them instead of their names.

Ryan Getzlaf was a key player for the **Anaheim Ducks**, leading them to a Stanley Cup in 2007 and becoming the franchise's all-time points leader with 1,019 points. His leadership and skill have left a lasting mark on the Ducks and their fans.

The Great Lakes Invitational is an annual college hockey tournament held in Michigan, featuring top college teams. It's known for intense competition and a holiday atmosphere, making it a beloved tradition in the Midwest hockey community.

Brian Leetch is one of the greatest American defensemen in NHL history, with over 1,000 points and a Conn Smythe Trophy. His combination of offensive talent and defensive skill made him a **New York Rangers** icon.

In Denmark, they have "disco hockey" nights where kids can play hockey while fun music plays and disco lights flash on the ice!

Nathan MacKinnon was drafted first overall by the **Colorado Avalanche** in 2013 and has since become one of the NHL's top players. His speed, skill, and 700 career points have made him a leader and fan favorite in Colorado.

Ron Hextall was known as one of the most fiery goalies, famous for being the first netminder to score a goal by shooting the puck into the opponent's net, now known as a "goalie goal." His aggressive style and competitive spirit left a lasting impression on the game.

The Beanpot Tournament is a famous college hockey event in Boston, featuring fierce rivalries between Boston University, Boston College, Northeastern, and Harvard. The tournament's intense games and passionate fans make it a key part of Boston's hockey culture.

The **Nashville Predators**' "Smashville" atmosphere is one of the rowdiest in the NHL, with fans known for their enthusiastic chants and catfish-throwing tradition. Their spirit has turned Nashville into a true hockey city and made Predators games unforgettable.

Patrice Bergeron has won the Selke Trophy as the NHL's best defensive forward five times, a league record. His commitment to both ends of the ice has made him a model of excellence and sportsmanship in the NHL.

Blake Wheeler, a former captain of the **Winnipeg Jets**, became the franchise's all-time points leader with over 800 points. Known for his leadership and strong play, Wheeler is a key figure in the Jets' modern history.

The Heritage Classic is an outdoor NHL game featuring Canadian teams, celebrating the country's hockey heritage. Played in scenic winter settings, the game has become a special event that connects the sport with its outdoor roots.

Carey Price achieved 361 career wins with the **Montreal Canadiens**, making him one of the winningest goalies in franchise history. His calm demeanor and incredible skill have made him a hero in Montreal and beyond.

The Japanese Ice Hockey Federation gives out special pink laces to all girls who join hockey - it's their way of saying "Welcome to the hockey family!"

Marcel Dionne, known as "Little Beaver," was one of the NHL's greatest scorers with 731 goals and 1,771 points. Despite never winning a Stanley Cup, Dionne's consistent excellence made him a Hall of Fame player.

A hockey net has exactly 252 square inches of space where you can score! That's why some people call it "finding the square inch."

David Pastrnak became one of the league's top scorers, with over 50 goals in the 2022-23 season. Known as "Pasta," his skill and charm have made him a fan favorite in Boston and a rising star in the league.

Saku Koivu, despite battling cancer, returned to the **Montreal Canadiens** and became a symbol of hope and resilience. His bravery and determination left a lasting impact on fans and fellow players.

Wayne Gretzky's 50 goals in 39 games in the 1981-82 season is a record that still stands, showcasing his unmatched scoring ability. This feat further solidified Gretzky's status as "The Great One."

Some players put baby powder in their skates before games to keep their feet dry. That's why sometimes you see little puffs of "smoke" when they take their skates off!

Darryl Sutter has coached teams to two Stanley Cup championships with the **Los Angeles Kings**, known for his unique coaching style and competitive spirit. His dedication to the game and calm under pressure have earned him respect across the NHL.

The World Junior Hockey Championship is a must-watch tournament for fans, showcasing the next generation of hockey stars. With passionate international rivalries, it's a thrilling way to see young players before they hit the NHL.

Jack Eichel was the first player from Boston University to be drafted in the NHL top two, becoming the face of the **Buffalo Sabres** and later the **Vegas Golden Knights**. Known for his elite skills, Eichel continues to impress fans with his high-level play.

The first organized women's hockey game was played in 1889 in Canada. They used tree branches as hockey sticks!

Dominik Hasek, known as "The Dominator," was one of the most unpredictable and acrobatic goalies in NHL history. With 389 wins, six Vezina Trophies, and two Hart Trophies, he redefined the position and remains an inspiration to goalies for his unique, unorthodox style.

Players used to use straight hockey sticks until **Stan Mikita** and **Bobby Hull** started curving their blades in the 1960s. They discovered by accident that curved sticks could make shots much harder to save.

Ken Morrow was a crucial part of both the 1980 "Miracle on Ice" U.S. Olympic team and the **New York Islanders** dynasty that won four straight Stanley Cups. Morrow's grit and defensive skill helped make him a rare four-time Stanley Cup champion and an Olympic gold medalist.

The **Kalamazoo Wings** dye their ice different colors for special games - they've used pink, green, and even rainbow ice!

Mike Modano, one of the greatest American-born players, retired with 1,374 points and won a Stanley Cup with the **Dallas Stars** in 1999. Known for his speed and smooth skating, Modano helped popularize hockey in the southern United States.

The "Legion of Doom" line for the **Philadelphia Flyers**, featuring **Eric Lindros, John LeClair,** and **Mikael Renberg,** was one of the most powerful lines of the 1990s. Their physicality and scoring ability made them a nightmare for defenders and a key part of the Flyers' success.

Roberto Luongo finished his career as one of the NHL's winningest goalies with 489 victories. Known for his sense of humor and consistent play, Luongo's legacy is felt strongly in Vancouver, where he led the **Canucks** to within one game of the Stanley Cup.

The **San Jose Sharks'** "Shark Head Entrance" is a unique pregame tradition where players skate through a giant shark head, pumping up the crowd. It's one of the coolest entrances in sports, adding excitement for fans and players alike!

The 1998 Nagano Olympics marked the first time NHL players participated, showcasing the best in the world.

Although Team Canada fell short, the tournament brought global attention to hockey and created unforgettable moments.

The **Buffalo Sabres**' "French Connection Line", with **Gilbert Perreault, Rick Martin,** and **Rene Robert**, was one of the most skilled and popular lines in the 1970s. Their chemistry and creativity made the Sabres a force to be reckoned with.

In Latvia, hockey is so popular that they built a special jail cell in their arena just for rowdy fans!

Patrick Roy's "Statue of Liberty" save in the 2002 playoffs was a flashy moment where he confidently held his glove high. Though it became memorable for different reasons, Roy's confidence epitomized his swagger and competitive spirit.

Mario Lemieux's five-goal "Five Different Ways" game in 1988 is one of hockey's greatest achievements. He scored at even strength, on a power play, short-handed, on a penalty shot, and into an empty net—all in one game!

◆

Hockey player **Mat Robinson,** a bronze medalist for Team Canada in the 2018 Olympics, practices stick handling by juggling tennis balls while riding a unicycle!

◆

Eddie Shore was known as one of hockey's toughest players, playing with numerous injuries and embodying the spirit of the old-time game. His intense play helped shape the identity of the **Boston Bruins** in their early years.

◆

The "Green Unit" was the legendary line of the Soviet Union's national team, made up of **Vladislav Tretiak, Viacheslav Fetisov, Alexei Kasatonov, Vladimir Krutov,** and **Sergei Makarov**. Known for their precision passing and chemistry, they were nearly unstoppable in the 1970s and '80s, dominating international tournaments.

The **South Carolina Stingrays** have fans who dress up as different sea creatures and sit in a special "aquarium section!"

Pekka Rinne became the first **Nashville Predators** goalie to score a goal in 2020. Known for his incredible reflexes and calm demeanor in the net, Rinne recorded over 350 wins in his career, becoming one of the Predators' most beloved players.

Ted Lindsay, one of the "Production Line" members of the **Detroit Red Wings**, helped establish the NHL Players' Association in 1957. Known for his fierce competitiveness and advocacy for players' rights, Lindsay changed the landscape of the sport, earning respect on and off the ice.

The "Lucky Loonie" story emerged during the 2002 Winter Olympics when a Canadian ice maker placed a loonie (Canadian dollar coin) at center ice for good luck. Canada's men's and women's teams won gold, and the loonie became a symbol of Canadian pride and superstition.

Evgeni Nabokov was the first NHL goalie to score a power-play goal, accomplishing the feat in 2002 while playing for the **San Jose Sharks**. Known for his aggressive style and quick glove, Nabokov became a fan favorite with over 350 wins in his career.

Bryan Trottier won six Stanley Cups as a player and was known for his balanced offense and physical play. With 524 goals and over 1,400 points, Trottier's skill and resilience led him to a Hall of Fame career with the **New York Islanders** and **Pittsburgh Penguins**.

Pierre Turgeon scored over 500 career goals and was known for his finesse and sportsmanship on the ice. Despite his immense skill, Turgeon won the Lady Byng

Trophy for sportsmanship, proving that players can be both competitive and respectful.

In 1988, fog actually formed INSIDE a hockey arena during a Stanley Cup Finals game! The Boston Garden was so hot and humid that players could barely see each other through the fog. They had to keep stopping the game to skate around and try to clear it!

Henri Richard, "The Pocket Rocket," won a record 11 Stanley Cups with the **Montreal Canadiens**. Known for his speed and tenacity, Richard became one of the most celebrated players in NHL history, playing with his brother, the legendary **Maurice Richard**, after whom the famous "Rocket" Richard Trophy is named.

The **Utah Hockey Club's** very first NHL draft pick was **Tij Iginla**, the son of legendary hockey star **Jarome Iginla**! Not only does Tij carry a famous hockey name, but he's already making waves as a player. It's like starting a new chapter of hockey history with a little family legacy twist.

The 2011 **Boston Bruins'** Stanley Cup victory was led by captain **Zdeno Chara** and goaltender **Tim Thomas**, who put up one of the best playoff performances in NHL history. Thomas earned the Conn Smythe Trophy for his .967 save percentage in the Finals, helping Boston secure its first Cup since 1972.

Zdeno Chara speaks seven languages and helped translate for new players on his team!

Rick Nash, one of the greatest **Columbus Blue Jackets**, retired with over 800 points and remains the franchise's all-time leader in goals. Known for his power-forward style and slick hands, Nash put Columbus on the hockey map.

The 2020 "Bubble Playoffs" saw teams play in isolated arenas in Toronto and Edmonton to safely complete the season during the COVID-19 pandemic. **Tampa Bay Lightning** emerged as the champions, while the unique setting and challenges made this a memorable playoff season.

"Hat Tricks" got their name from a Canadian tradition of tossing hats on the ice to celebrate a player scoring three goals in one game. This fun ritual continues around the world, with fans tossing all kinds of hats to honor the player's achievement.

Connor McDavid's 105-point season in 2020-21, despite it being a shortened 56-game season, was one of the most remarkable feats in modern NHL history. Known for his speed and skill, McDavid's points-per-game average was the highest since **Mario Lemieux's** prime.

◆

Trevor Zegras, known for his jaw-dropping "Michigan goal" and assists, brings creativity and flash to the NHL. His fearless approach to scoring has inspired young players to try bold moves and push the boundaries of what's possible on the ice.

The "Michigan Goal" in ice hockey is a creative and tricky move where a player scores by scooping the puck up onto their stick and then lifting it into the net from behind the goalie. It was first pulled off by a player named **Mike Legg** during a college hockey game for the University of Michigan in 1996, which is why it's called the "Michigan." The move takes a lot of skill and balance and has become famous because it's rare and really exciting to see!

◆

The **Hershey Bears'** "Teddy Bear Toss" tradition involves fans throwing thousands of teddy bears onto the ice after the team's first goal. The bears are then donated to local charities, making this a beloved holiday tradition that combines hockey with giving back.

◆

Sergei Gonchar was one of the NHL's most productive defensemen, finishing with over 800 points. Known for his offensive prowess, Gonchar played a crucial role in the **Pittsburgh Penguins'** 2009 Stanley Cup win.

Mike Richter, one of the best American goaltenders, helped the **New York Rangers** win the 1994 Stanley Cup. Known for his agility and athleticism, Richter remains a beloved figure in Rangers' history.

The "Battle of Alberta" rivalry between the **Edmonton Oilers** and **Calgary Flames** is one of the most intense in hockey. Known for its high-scoring games and physical play, this rivalry has created many unforgettable moments for fans!

Did you know hockey players can lose up to 5-10 pounds of sweat during a single game? That's why they drink so much water!

One of the funniest stories about a hockey stick breaking during a professional game involves legendary goalie **Patrick Roy**. During a game, Roy tried to clear the puck from behind his net but accidentally broke his stick on the boards. Without missing a beat, he picked up the broken shaft and skated nonchalantly back to the crease, attempting to use it as though nothing had happened. The comedic sight of a goalie wielding half a stick left fans and commentators laughing.

As a bonus, here's three truly inspiring stories about hockey fans just like you. Remember, the greatest players started out as beginners, and you may one day be in a book just like this! Work hard, believe in yourself, and don't let anything stand in the way of your dreams!

In 2018, Alex Luey was an 11-year-old hockey player from Niagara Falls, Ontario who caught the attention of NHL superstar **Alex Ovechkin**. Two years earlier, Alex Luey had been diagnosed with bone cancer in his right leg. After intense treatment and surgery to remove part of his leg bone, doctors weren't sure if he'd ever play hockey again.

But young Alex was determined. He went through months of physical therapy and practiced endlessly to regain his strength and skating ability. Not only did he return to playing hockey, but he became his team's captain.

When Ovechkin heard Alex's story, he was so impressed that he invited Alex to a **Toronto Maple Leafs vs. Washington Capitals** game. Ovechkin promised Alex he would try to score for him. That night, Ovechkin didn't just score one goal - he scored three, completing a hat trick! After each goal, Ovechkin pointed up to where Alex was watching in the stands.

After the game, Ovechkin gave Alex his stick and jersey from the game. But more importantly, Alex Luey's story showed kids everywhere that with enough determination, you can overcome huge obstacles and get back to doing what you love.

Today, Alex continues to inspire others by sharing his story and showing that cancer couldn't keep him away from the sport he loves.

◆

Jonathan Pitre wasn't a professional hockey player, but his story is deeply connected to the sport. Born with Epidermolysis Bullosa (EB), a rare and painful skin condition that made even the slightest touch feel like burning, Jonathan couldn't play hockey like other kids. However, his love for the game and his determination made him a symbol of courage for hockey fans everywhere.

Jonathan became a hockey ambassador, inspiring teams and players with his positivity and resilience. His favorite team, the **Ottawa Senators**, treated him like one of their own. He signed a one-day contract with the team, met players, and even gave motivational speeches. Despite his challenges, Jonathan never gave up on his dreams or his love for hockey.

Although Jonathan passed away in 2018, his story continues to inspire young hockey fans to stay strong and never give up, no matter the obstacles. He showed that you don't have to play the game to embody the spirit of hockey – teamwork, bravery, and determination are what truly matter.

Tij Iginla was a 12-year-old player in Calgary who faced repeated racial harassment during his youth hockey games in 2020. Instead of letting the cruel comments discourage him, Tij focused on becoming an even better player, supported by his father, former NHL star **Jarome Iginla**. But what makes this story special is what happened next. When other young players in the league heard about what Tij was experiencing, they started standing up for him. His teammates and even players from other teams began speaking out against racism whenever they heard it. They wore special tape on their sticks to show support, and many parents and coaches used it as a teaching moment to discuss respect and inclusion in hockey.

Tij continued to excel at hockey, becoming one of the top players in his age group. Like his father (who was the first Black captain in NHL history and is now in the Hockey Hall of Fame), Tij showed that character and skill matter more than anything else.

In 2023, Tij was selected first overall in the WHL Bantam Draft - the same league where his father had starred years before. His story helped change attitudes in youth hockey and showed how young players can make their sport better for everyone.

The best part? Tij didn't just overcome the challenges - he and his supporters helped make hockey more welcoming for other kids who might face similar situations. His story reminds us that sometimes the biggest victories happen off the ice when players stand together to make the game better for everyone.

We sincerely hope you enjoyed this book! Our goal is create fun, engaging content for all ages, with a focus on positivity, growth, and inspiration.

If you loved this book, please consider leaving us a review! You can do so simply by navigating to the books page using the QR Code below. We sure appreciate it!

Thanks again and we'll see you in the future!